Automata and Mechanical Toys

With Illustrations and Text by Britain's Leading Makers, and Photographs and Plans for Making Mechanisms

Rodney Peppé

The Crowood Press

First published in 2002 by
The Crowood Press Ltd
Ramsbury, Marlborough
Wiltshire SN8 2HR

British Library Cataloguing-in-Publication Data
A catalogue record for this book is available from the
British Library.

ISBN 1 86126 510 7

Typeset and designed by
D & N Publishing
Baydon, Marlborough, Wiltshire.

Printed and bound in Singapore by Craft Print International Ltd.

CONTENTS

Acknowledgements 4

Credits and Permissions 4

List of Contributors 5

Preface 7

Introduction 8

Chapter 1   A Brief History of Automata and Mechanical Toys   10

Chapter 2   The Origins of Contemporary Automata   29

Chapter 3   Tools and Materials   49

Chapter 4   Techniques   63

Chapter 5   Making Automata Mechanisms   77

Chapter 6   Theme Projects   126

Chapter 7   Design   141

Chapter 8   Painting and Finishing   154

Bibliography 157

Index 158

For Georgia and Blair.

ACKNOWLEDGEMENTS

A book of this type would not have been possible without the generous co-operation of the makers in supplying illustrations of their work and accompanying text. To them I offer my warm thanks and appreciation for allowing me to reproduce their contributions.

My sincere thanks are also due to Fleur Hitchcock and Ian McKay of Hitchcocks', Bath, for recommending me to The Crowood Press. I am indebted to them for allowing me to use Hitchcocks' list of makers' names and addresses, which simplified a difficult task.

Finally, I would like to thank Tatjana, my wife, for typing the manuscript and helping me through what has been the most enjoyable book I have ever produced.

Rodney Peppé

CREDITS AND PERMISSIONS

pp37–9, 73–5 © photos: Heini Schneebeli
p77 Cabaret Mechanical Theatre

John Grayson
pp25–6, 27 (top right) & 27 (bottom)
© photos: A. Yale
p27 (top left) © photo: G. Murrel

Peter Markey
pp61, 77 Timber Kits Ltd

Keith Newstead
pp73–5 © photos: Heini Schneebeli
Cabaret Mechanical Theatre

Rodney Peppé
pp4, 6, 9, 12, 16, 17 (three photos), 23,

31–4, 36, 43 (right), 106, 160, Author's
Collection
p9 © photo: V. Oliver

Robert Race
pp120–2 © photos: Thalia Race

Paul Spooner
pp132–3 © photos: Heini Schneebeli
p77 Cabaret Mechanical Theatre

*Automata Mechanisms, Plans,
Diagrams and Drawings*
pp76, 78–110, 112–13, 160
Drawn and made by the author

LIST OF CONTRIBUTORS

Lucy Casson	20–2
Ron Fuller	22–4
John Grayson	25–7
Neil Hardy	40–2
Andy Hazell	43–5
Tim Hunkin	46–8
John Maltby	55–7
Tony Mann	58–60
Peter Markey	60–2
Ian McKay	67–9
Frank Nelson	70–2
Keith Newstead	73–5
Rodney Peppé	117–19
Robert Race	120–2
Martin Smith	123–5
Paul Spooner	131–3
Melanie Tomlinson	134–6
Douglas Wilson	137–9
Kristy Wyatt Smith	145–7
Vicki Wood	148–50
Jan Zalud	151–3

PREFACE

If this book has a main purpose it is to encourage beginners and intermediate students to make their own automata and mechanical toys. But it is also aimed at enthusiasts and collectors who, for the first time, are offered the opportunity to read about modern makers and see a good selection of their work – five pictures each – in one book. Until now, only exhibition catalogues showing one or two pieces by automatists have been available, and those have been few and far between. Without the generosity and co-operation of the contributors in supplying textual and visual material, publication would have been virtually impossible. They *are* the book. Their contribution provides the chance for an appraisal of their work, not as a group, but as a set of highly gifted individuals – a band of different drummers, each marching to their own tune.

A large part of the book covers the main mechanisms used in the building of automata and mechanical toys. Step-by-step instructions, with photographs, cutting guides and instructions, will help readers to make their own automata. The practical guidance also includes advice on making bearings and shafts, cams and followers, cranks, linkages, ratchets, drives, gears and levers. All the mechanisms can be made in a piece, which can be assembled and dismantled by using friction-fitting pegs.

The book also includes a brief history of automata and mechanical toys, culminating in the hiatus that separated the craftsmen engineers of the eighteenth and nineteenth centuries from the artist craftsmen of the 1970s. There is a chapter on the emergence of seminal artists in the medium, Alexander Calder, Jean Tinguely and Sam Smith, sometimes referred to as the father of modern automata. The appearance of Cabaret Mechanical Theatre in 1983, under the auspices of its founder Sue Jackson, is described as a landmark of the contemporary automata scene. Her encouragement of Peter Markey, Paul Spooner and Ron Fuller started in motion a ball that is still rolling. The chapter on design is devoted to these three CMT automatists, who have influenced their fellow makers for more than twenty years. Frank Nelson separately forged his own path under the championship of the late Sam Smith, who also encouraged Peter Markey in his endeavours. This is how the seeds of contemporary automata were sown.

Alongside the general history of the subject, there are individual stories from the makers themselves. Chapter 6, on theme projects, encourages students to make their own pieces on a theme of their own choosing, and there are also the inevitable (but very useful) chapters on tools, materials, techniques, painting and finishing, offering vital practical information.

I hope the reader extracts from these pages some of the joy I experienced in writing and devising them, and appreciates the rich offerings of the various makers. I feel privileged to have been entrusted to showcase their work in a more durable form than has hitherto been available. If learning about mechanisms and seeing the work of leading makers encourages students to make their way in this fascinating field, I will have succeeded in my aim.

OPPOSITE PAGE:
'A Different Drummer' (Rodney Peppé), powered automaton using a fishing reel mechanism to move the harlequin drummer differentially out of rank, 1991 (248mm × 191mm × 95mm/9¾ × 7½ × 3¾in).

INTRODUCTION

People are often puzzled about the meaning of the word 'automata', but they usually know what a 'mechanical toy' is, and many have fond memories of a favourite wind-up animal or human figure. Do automata bear any resemblance to those wind-up toys? The answer is that they do indeed – only more so. Automata are distinguished from mechanical toys by the cycle and complexity of their movement. The mechanical toy is a child's plaything; the automaton is an adult's plaything. It is a fascinating object, to be demonstrated to others by its owner, and a magical reflection of its maker's ingenuity.

The word 'automaton' has been defined as a piece of mechanism with *concealed* motive power, but this definition is somewhat dated, since many automatists now believe in revealing the mechanism as part of the performance. In most cases, definitions of automata do not really help, because the pieces differ so much in their mechanical and artistic aspirations. Sculpture, unless it is kinetic or mobile, is easier to define because it is static, but 'mechanical sculpture' fails to describe automata adequately. Clearly, a new word is needed.

In its singular form, 'automaton' tends to evoke a Frankenstein-like creature with a high forehead and a bolt through its neck. The pictures of makers' work in these pages will offer a better understanding of the term 'automata' than any words. The common denominator in these pieces is a subversive sense of humour combined with a rather British sense of the ridiculous, which has its roots in Heath Robinson, Rowland Emett, Bruce Lacey and Michael Bentine, among others. Added to this is, of course, mechanical ingenuity. Each piece extends an invitation to interaction. The viewer is often mirrored in the piece he handles and amused by its ability to mock him and his surroundings.

Above all, 'automatry' does not take itself too seriously, ensuring its enduring charm, and modestly denies any status as Art with a capital 'A'. But it may be nudging its way towards becoming an art form. Where industry once exclusively commissioned sculptors and mural painters to enhance its public spaces, it is now turning to automatists, or to artists who work with engineers, to build pieces that interact with the observer. Twenty years ago, the late Sam Smith was commissioned by renowned graphic design group Pentagram to devise an animated display of puppets reflecting the people of Lewisham in their Riverdale Shopping Centre. (Sadly, this has disappeared, as the cost of maintenance was too high to sustain its continued existence.) In the mid-1980s, the painter Kit Williams (of *Masquerade* fame) was commissioned to design and build, with the aid of engineers, the automated clock in Cheltenham's Regent Arcade. The clock is a wonderful talking point for shoppers and visitors, giving a focal point to the arcade. It is constantly entertaining, but especially as it strikes the the quarters and the hours. At noon, a giant fish blows bubbles as the animation reaches its peak.

The latest notable commission is 'Cornucopia', designed and built by Paul Spooner, in collaboration with Will Jackson, for the Tropics Biome of the Eden Project in Cornwall. This fully automated exhibit, which took six months to design, build and install, shows how natural products from rainforests the world over are turned into everyday household objects. The message is a reminder of the countless products used from rainforest materials, and of the significance of the vital resource that supplies them. It must be heartening for the public in general – and automatists in particular – for 'Cornucopia' to be seen in such a successful venue as the Eden Project. The hope is that industrial designers and architects will be inspired to think in terms of powered automata, rather than static sculpture and murals, when advising industry on the decoration of foyers and courtyards (mechanical maintenance notwithstanding).

The place of modern automata and mechanical toys in the technological age is difficult to gauge. The memory of a chip can outperform a cam's a millionfold, yet it cannot reproduce that magical quirkiness that is the hallmark of modern automata. In the future, who knows whether automata will be totally governed by computer technology, or whether the 'rude mechanicals' (as Frank Nelson describes his own automata) will survive? And if they do survive, will they continue on the paths laid down by Calder, Tinguely, Sam Smith and CMT, or will they branch out into something quite different, as unrelated to them as they themselves are to the Victorian automatists?

Time will tell. In the interim, many young automatists in art schools, as yet unencumbered by the baggage of technology, are producing lively, imaginative work. Popular with students, Tim Hunkin is one automatist who has been involved in corporate commissions; perhaps his experiences will inspire young artists to channel their own energies in a similar direction. With more realistic prices being paid for corporate work than in galleries, their work for collectors could, to some extent, be subsidized. Industry is being presented with a golden opportunity to enliven its cultural facade by utilizing their talents.

'Hand-cranked Drummer', by Rodney Peppé.

1 A BRIEF HISTORY OF AUTOMATA AND MECHANICAL TOYS

AUTOMATA

Earliest Days

The notion of man-made man has exercised human ingenuity from far back into prehistory. There is evidence that, while developing language and tools and executing cave paintings, prehistoric man was also making models of himself, with movable limbs. In ancient Egypt, special jointed statues of the gods were secretly manipulated by priests, so that they appeared to be moving and speaking of their own accord. These manifestations of 'life' were used to exercise power over underlings, and were the beginning of the link between automata and religious control through the ages.

The first recorded automata appeared in Egypt in the second or third century BC. The renowned engineers Ctesibius (who developed the rack and pinion movement and the self-regulating clock), Philo the Byzantian and Hero of Alexandria (285–222BC) all belonged to the Alexandrian School, along with other learned alumni, Euclid and Archimedes. It was Hero, one of Ctesibius' pupils, who recorded the work of his predecessors, and, indeed, his own inventions, expressing them in mechanical form by making models. He used the models to entertain his pupils, thereby teaching them about the physical laws that related to the workings of the models. The theorems devised by Hero of Alexandria that governed these working models survive in his treatise on *pneumatica*. Among other things, he built a machine called an *eolipile*, to show the expansion of gas when heated and the

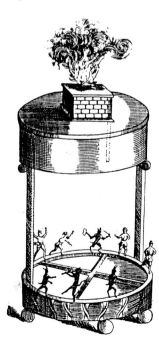

The steam eolipile of Hero of Alexandria.

force of the gas escaping from various orifices. The lateral tubes (not shown in the illustration) were connected to a freely revolving platform that supported little figures. The machine was simply a turntable driven by reaction.

The knowledge that the ancient Greeks possessed about gears, simple mechanisms, hydraulics and pneumatics formed the basis of mechanical science for later civilizations, reaching the Byzantine world after the fall of Rome (AD 476). The Byzantines drew upon the legacy, making water clocks that incorporated automata, and the inevitable war machines. They and the Muslim rulers revelled in the wonderful mechanical displays, which had now reached a high point of ingenuity. The accumulated knowledge travelled to the Arab world and, from the seventh century AD, Islamic artisans led the field, creating even more elaborate animated water clocks and ways of recording time.

The monumental clocks of the Arab world, incorporating spectacular automata, were far more advanced than the weight-driven clocks being used in Europe at the same time. However, by the fourteenth century, automata had begun to appear on colossal cathedral clocks in many European cities. The animated figures that struck the hours were called *Jaquemarts*, or 'Jacks'. They were made of painted wrought iron, generally portrayed as a mechanically operated man who used a hammer to strike the hours. Later, the striking of the halves and quarters was added, incorporating more automata. In addition to their striking duties, the figures would also enact religious or profane scenes, much to the amusement of the public and giving rise to mixed feelings on the part of the Church, which hoped that such displays would mostly inspire devotion.

During the Middle Ages, all mechanical science had been regarded with suspicion and was often confused with black magic. An awkward relationship had developed between the Church and the automatists. As the focus of learning moved away from the monasteries to the newly established universities, however, scientists were able to experiment more freely. Bavarian philosopher Albertus Magnus (*c.* 1200) was said to have constructed a mechanical man of brass who could speak, while Roger Bacon (1214–98), the English monk who has been called the father of experimental science, explored similar projects, undeterred by the teachings of the past. St Thomas Aquinas, a former pupil of Albertus Magnus, was one religious figure who clung to monastic bigotry; he smashed his former master's mechanical companion, denouncing it as the work of the devil. Albertus Magnus was devastated: 'Thus perishes the work of thirty years,' he lamented.

A Golden Age

In the sixteenth century, Hero of Alexandria's treatise on *pneumatica* was translated into Latin and subsequently into Italian and German. The writings and drawings were pounced upon by the Renaissance engineers, who constructed amazing water gardens complete with hydraulic automata. The gardens of Villa d'Este and Pratolino in Italy, for example, drew visitors from all over Europe, including Solomon de Caus (1576–1626), a French engineer who had studied the technical heritage of the ancient automatists. De Caus brought grottoes and mechanical hydraulic effects to Stuart England. In the grottoes, articulated mythological statuary – deities, satyrs and various other creatures – were constructed to play

practical jokes on hapless visitors, who were drenched in water, or covered in salt, or, even worse, soot! The mischievous humour was very 'Renaissance' but the mechanics at the heart of the constructions had clearly been handed down by the Ancient Greeks. Increasingly ingenious creations appeared, which were breathtaking in their mimicry of life.

Descartes and other philosophers of the Renaissance had played their part in dispelling prejudice and misconceptions about mechanical devices, but religious paranoia persisted even into the eighteenth century. A number of diehards continued to condemn as pagan magic all mechanical things, especially those that bore an uncanny resemblance to life.

The most famous automatist of the eighteenth century was Jacques de Vaucanson (1709–82), a native of Grenoble in France. He entered training for the priesthood, but his stay at the college was short-lived; during his time there, he made some flying angel automata that were destroyed by the Jesuit priests for their 'heresy'. De Vaucanson took this as a cue to relieve himself of his vows, and went on to lead a rather wild life in Paris, working his way through a small fortune left to him by his father. After studying music, medicine and mechanics, de Vaucanson began to earn a living from exhibiting his automata. His most famous creation was a life-sized mechanical duck made of gilt brass, with flexible rubber tubing to simulate intestines. The duck not only looked like a duck and quacked like a duck but, on being fed corn, it also digested and produced droppings like a duck! In later life, de Vaucanson followed a more sober and distinguished path as Inspector of Mechanical Inventions at the Royal Academy of Sciences, and achieved recognition as one of the most significant minds in the development of automata.

Automata in human form became known as 'androids'. Produced by de Vaucanson, and other masters such as Jacquet-Droz,

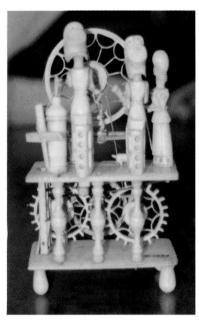

Front and rear views of French POW model in Peterborough Museum.

OPPOSITE PAGE:
Nineteenth-century automata were characterized by emotional idealism and paid homage to the entertainers of the day. They were expensive, even after the introduction of low-cost methods of production, and were not intended for children.

Leschot and Maillardet, these figures perfectly reproduced the human movements of drawing, writing or playing an instrument. The pieces were jewels of complex mechanical invention, requiring long and painstaking work, and automatists would complete relatively few pieces in a lifetime. Their main purpose was to imitate life by mechanical means; only today's robots could match their ingenuity, but nothing could match their style.

Following a series of naval victories during the Napoleonic wars, thousands of French prisoners filled British prisons. The skilled craftsmen, watchmakers, clockmakers and jewellers among them would supplement their meagre rations by selling their own work in the prison's market. Materials were limited, but there were plenty of bones from the cookhouse, which explains why so many of the pieces were tiny and white (although many were painted). Guillotines were popular subjects, as were domestic and trading activities, such as spinning, cobbling and knife-grinding. The delicacy of the wheels that drove some of models must have involved painstaking cutting work, but time was hardly at a premium for these

craftsmen of quality. Some escapees managed to earn enough from their work to buy a passage back to France.

As the industrial age dawned, the French seemed reluctant to surrender their artistic traditions to new technology. During the second part of the nineteenth century, however, trains and steamships had an enormous effect on travel and communications, and the establishment of the new department stores affected the automata and mechanical toys industry. Artist-craftsmen were taken by surprise at the speed of developments, and totally unprepared for the surge in demand.

The day of the expensive 'one-off' automaton was gone. Prices came down as production lines were developed to make numbers of identical pieces, supplying a middle class who had prospered in the improved financial climate, and liked to display the mechanical marvels in their drawing rooms. The growing popularity of automata allowed inventors to exercise their ingenuity and flights of fancy, profiting from modern economical methods of manufacture that none the less allowed them to retain some of the quality of a hand-made product. As the automata industry grew, so did competition. Innovation was all that mattered in the new, competitive market, and wholesale plagiarism was rife. The tiniest new detail would persuade a buyer to choose one automaton over another. So fierce was the rivalry between firms that many eschewed registering patents to protect their inventions, preferring to guard their originality by constant change rather than relying on time-consuming legislation.

Some wonderful new effects were introduced in a Golden Age that lasted from the mid-1800s to the beginning of the First World War. Leading makers such as Bontems, Lambert, Phalibois, Renou, Roullet et Decamps, Théroude and Vichy influenced and were influenced by each other's creations.

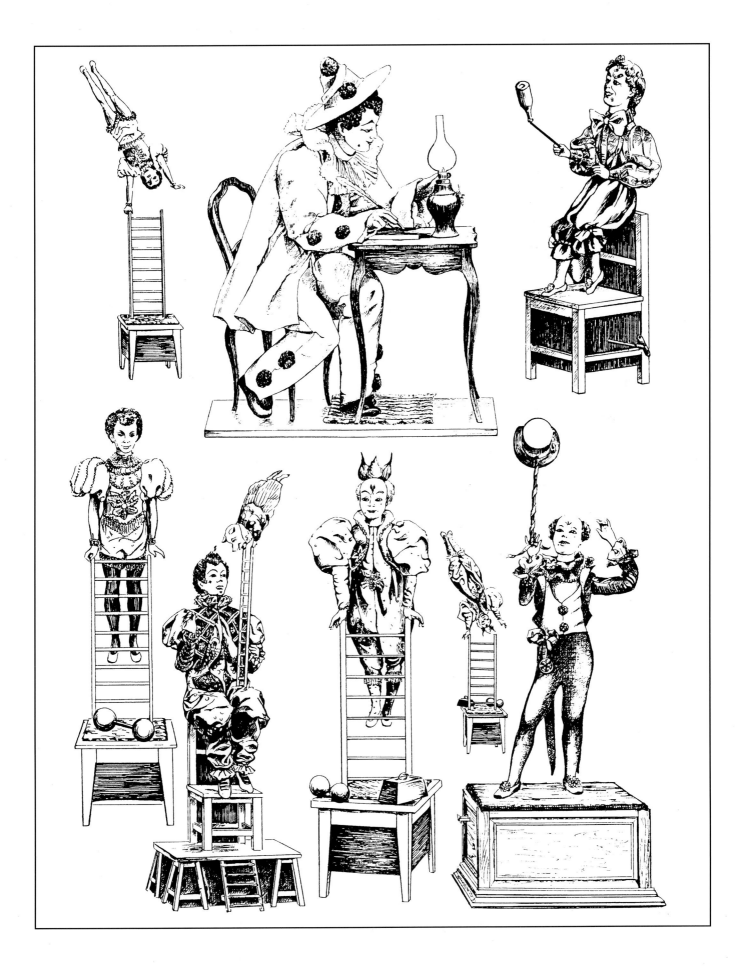

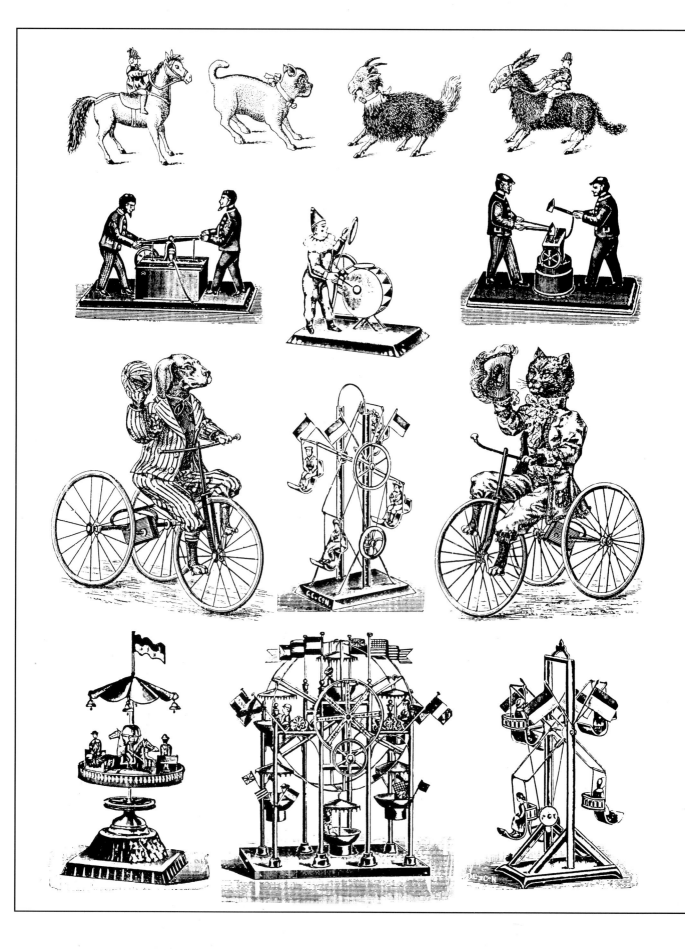

The nineteenth-century automatist was a clockmaker by training who, with his own expertise and that of craftsmen and artisans skilled in turning, drilling and cutting, oversaw the assembly of all the diverse components that made up a piece. The making process began with the modelling of a clay or wax figure from which a mould was made to form the head, body and limbs. The working mechanism and musical movement were inserted in the completed body before the finishing touches were added by painters, seamstresses and hairdressers.

These automata were usually displayed in the children's section in exhibitions, but they were not for children. In spite of cheaper production methods, costs increased as they became increasingly sophisticated and more lifelike. Many aimed to reflect Parisian society of the day, capturing the essence of performances by famous entertainers, clowns, acrobats and music hall stars. Just as they mirrored the society that created them, so were they subject to changing fashions. Around the 1890s they were thrust into a new role, on public display in department store windows, extolling the virtues of the store's products by their gestures. They became larger, in order to attract shoppers, and the musical accompaniment was dispensed with as it could not be heard from the other side of a window. The commercial automaton came to outshine its domestic counterpart, and what was once the exclusive property of the well-to-do now became available to all.

Decline

By the end of the First World War, electrical automata replaced the clockwork models in the elaborate window displays. Clockwork could only run for several minutes, but the action on an electrical piece could run on an ever repeating cycle until the power was switched off. Demand for clockwork automata diminished and they fell into decline.

In a fast-developing world it became increasingly difficult to find skilled craftsmen and engineers to build them.

The decline was accelerated when US importation laws placed an embargo on French toys coming into the USA. To beat the legislation, certain French firms sent foremen from their workshops to set up on the other side of the Atlantic, but automata were, it seemed, destined to disappear. During the First World War, France itself banned exportation of toys and this brought production to a virtual halt.

After the horrors of the conflict, the public was in no mood to return to pre-war luxuries, as automata were perceived to be. As the twentieth century settled into the Jazz Age, with its new amusements – the gramophone, the wireless and moving pictures – the extinction of automata was virtually complete. Only mechanical toys, which were in certain cases scaled-down versions of their superior relations, continued to flourish. They had a mass appeal, were affordable and in tune with the times, and they endure today.

MECHANICAL TOYS

The main factors distinguishing mechanical toys from automata are running time and the number of cams. Automata were programmed to execute a series of complicated movements within a time span. The duration and complexity of the cycle distinguished them from the simpler mechanical toys.

Origins

France was supreme in the manufacture of automata in the nineteenth century, but it was makers in Germany, the centre of tinplate production, who produced the finest mechanical toys before the First World War. Production quality was high, with manufacturers such as Bing, Carette (an expatriate Frenchman), Lehmann and Marklin showing meticulous attention to detail.

OPPOSITE PAGE:
Nineteenth-century mechanical toys were characterized by ingenuity and style, although the craftsmen who made them were rewarded with very low wages. They owed their continued success to the fact that they were able to keep pace with changing markets.

Before the development of tinplate, early mechanical toys (at the beginning of the nineteenth century) were made of wood and sometimes fabric, with very simple mechanisms, perhaps involving a single lever or cam. Few of these have survived – they were cheap toys for the general market, and made with perishable materials. They depicted subjects such as figures spinning or playing a drum, horses and carts, jumping jacks, acrobats, and the like. Leather strips or springs served for joints while string and wire levers were used to operate the simple mechanisms. A typical toy was a drummer, with movable arms attached at the shoulder by strings that were wound round dowel rods connected eccentrically between three rollers. Turning the handle produced a drumming action in alternating rhythm.

In 1842, the reduction of the rate of duty on French toys had a drastic effect on the British toy trade, cutting earnings by half. (At this time, French mechanical toys were also superior to the British ones and dealers made handsome profits on them and other foreign imports from Germany and Switzerland.) With so little margin for profit, copying and counter-copying of inventions were rife. Even one of the best of the French makers, Fernand Martin, at the height of his career, was accused of plagiarism by other toymakers. Some claimed that he had purchased their ideas (paying a pittance), but they were particularly annoyed by the fact that he claimed ideas as his own when submitting pieces for exhibitions. Whatever the truth, his factory, which opened in Paris in 1880, was the most successful in Europe. He employed over 200 workers, and had his own tinplate foundry and separate departments undertaking die stamping, soldering and assembly, painting and hairdressing. A production line of nimble-fingered girls ensured that the little mechanical figures, which were skeletal in form, were dressed in appropriate national dress for sale at home or abroad. They were cheap, mass-produced toys and, before the First World War,

daily production totals were as high as 8,000. Despite these figures, relatively few examples of the toys exist today, at least outside collections and auction houses.

The origins of the US toy trade were very different from those in Europe. The USA absorbed the skills and traditions of British, Irish, German, Italian, Dutch and Scandinavian settlers, which all went into the melting pot to become, collectively, 'American folk art'. It was upon this tradition that American mechanical toys were based. In the best sense, the tradition was amateur since the exponents were not professional makers. Their naivety is evident in the early nineteenth-century toys, which are crudely fashioned and employ very basic mechanisms – for example, a jumping jack would use a simple central pull string to activate the arms and legs (see the photo left).

Through the years, the folk art tradition was also strongly present in the making of whirligigs, which originated in Germany and Holland. They were made as animated weathervanes with arm paddles to catch the wind, if they were figures, or propellers, and proved to be the forerunners of many hand-cranked toys.

In England, Prince Albert provided a marvellous fillip to the toy trade by introducing the Christmas tree and present-giving to his adopted country in the 1840s. Determined to celebrate Christmas in his own German way, the Prince Consort unwittingly forged the first strong links between the religious holiday and commerce. The new tradition of offering toys as gifts gave joy not only to the English children who received them, but also to the toymakers who made them. The extra seasonal income provided hitherto unknown financial security for many impecunious toymakers, who were extremely poorly paid for their labour-intensive work. They were the ones who made the 'fancy toys' (as mechanical toys were termed by the trade), but they often had to invent new toys, too. Invention was an activity for idle periods.

A version of an early American jumping jack (Rodney Peppé), 1999 (280mm × 152mm × 67mm/11 × 6 × 2⅝in).

Common Mechanisms

A number of principles and simple mechanisms were used by inventors to govern their creations, ranging from the use of wind and water, handed down by the Ancient Greeks, to other motive forces, such as gravity allowing sand to fall into a hopper, activating a small figure or scene. The sand toy, employing the combined principles of the hourglass and millwheel, is one example using this method. Motive power was also provided by escapements using marbles, or lead shot placed within balancing tubes. Flywheels regulated the speed of clockwork in toys in which the motor had to be slowed down, such as the popular 'living picture'.

Popular in the 1890s, 'living pictures', or 'clockwork tableaux', as they were also known, were really an extension of the sand toy, but used clockwork instead. This drove the cams, which operated levers joined by delicate threads to animate the picture. One example, made in Germany, shows singing kittens and their music teacher, based on a scene by illustrator Louis Wain. There is also a musical version, framed identically, of a Louis Wain cat and dog band. 'Living pictures' were first introduced into the USA by Albert

Choral kittens opening and closing their mouths, twitching their tails and music sheets, while their teacher waves his baton and sings along with them. This piece was mass-produced in Germany in the 1890s (254 × 356 × 121mm/10 × 14 × 4¾in).

BELOW LEFT: The back view shows the clock movement with a card flywheel to slow down the action. A wooden pulley, inserted in the movement, operates the driveband around the large cam, with pins, which works tiny wire levers attached by threads to other levers, which activate the 'living picture'.

BELOW: Hand-coloured print 'A New Year's Song', drawn by Louis Wain for the Boys Own Paper, *upon which the 'living picture' is based.*

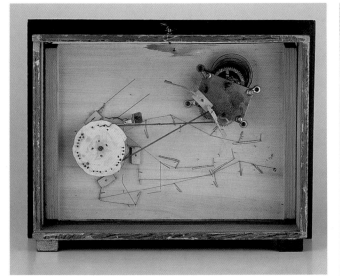

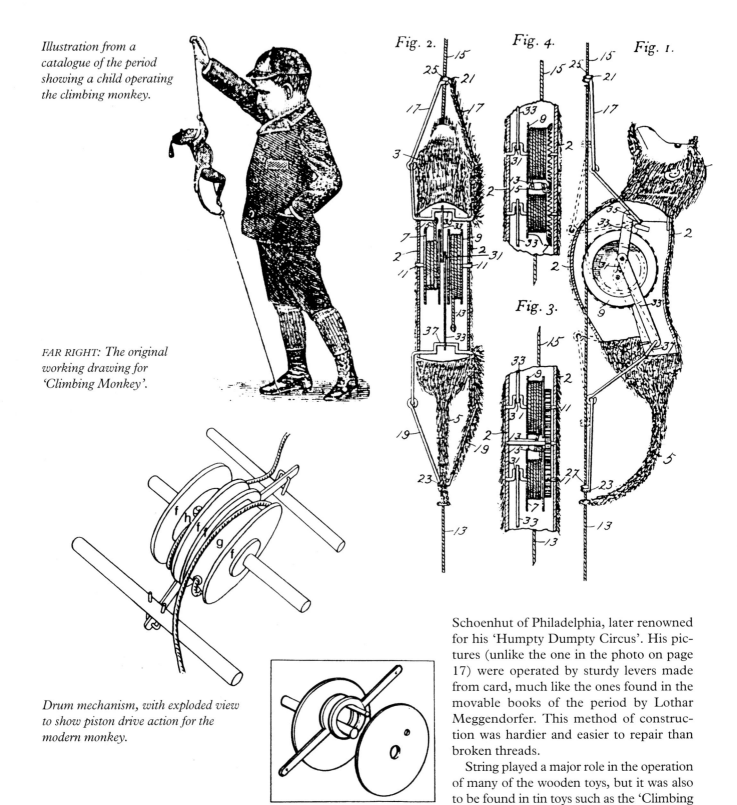

Illustration from a catalogue of the period showing a child operating the climbing monkey.

FAR RIGHT: *The original working drawing for 'Climbing Monkey'.*

Fig. 2. Fig. 4. Fig. 1.

Fig. 3.

Drum mechanism, with exploded view to show piston drive action for the modern monkey.

Schoenhut of Philadelphia, later renowned for his 'Humpty Dumpty Circus'. His pictures (unlike the one in the photo on page 17) were operated by sturdy levers made from card, much like the ones found in the movable books of the period by Lothar Meggendorfer. This method of construction was hardier and easier to repair than broken threads.

String played a major role in the operation of many of the wooden toys, but it was also to be found in tin toys such as the 'Climbing

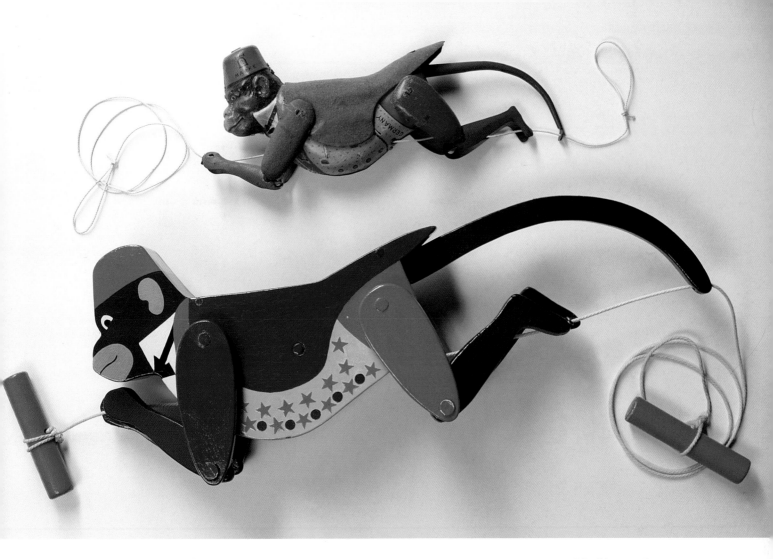

Monkey'. This ingenious mechanism was invented by Fernand Strauss of Minneapolis and later copied by the German firm Lehmann. The antique monkey shown on page 18 is a 1903 Lehmann toy, while the larger version above was made by the author to see how the mechanism worked.

Fernand Strauss called himself the 'Toy King' and was the principal manufacturer of wind-up toys in the early part of the twentieth century. Unlike the sturdier clockwork toys, wind-ups were fitted with feeble spring mechanisms and were very light in construction. They were most ingenious, and remain so to this day. Strauss owned factories and retail shops and was able to benefit, like other firms, when toys made in Germany became unpopular after the war.

The following years saw a great interest in transport toys, reflecting continuing developments in technology. As each new ship, train, balloon or aeroplane made its debut, its toy version would soon follow. Tinplate transport toys became a vast part of the market, and a subject of their own, generating much interesting literature.

The history of mechanical toys is a continuing one, for they have survived social upheaval and changing fashions. Whereas automata were priced out of the market by their own excellence, exclusivity, rising labour costs and changing tastes, mechanical toys have managed to keep pace with the vicissitudes of fluctuating markets and unpredictable trends. Today, mechanical toys command an important position in the saleroom. If their prices, especially for tinplate, are anything to go by, their appeal to the collector is undiminished.

Climbing monkeys (Rodney Peppé collection), antique and modern. The smaller is the 1903 tinplate original by Lehmann. The larger version was made by Rodney Peppé in 1978. Both employ the same double drum mechanism (see diagram opposite).

'Here We Go, Here We Go, Here We Go' by Lucy Casson, 1983.

MAKERS' WORK

Lucy Casson

I started making automata out of tin and wire while I was working at a textile mill. I think the looms were more inspiring than the weaving, not that the mechanisms I made were anything like looms.

I developed very simple cams and movements. They had to be simple because they were so wobbly. A few bent pieces of wire became a person wildly drinking tea, or some wildebeest galloping like a flapping headscarf in the wind.

I liked the way people took part in the work by turning the handle, getting satisfaction from the simplest mechanisms. Despite this world full of technology, there is still wonder in some wobbly pieces of wire and bits of tin-can construction – waving or swimming, or frying some eggs on a tiny oven. Every scene is accompanied by the sounds of tin clanking and grinding.

'Ronald Reagan Bulldozer', 1986.

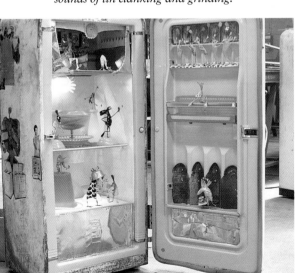

'Fridge', 2000.

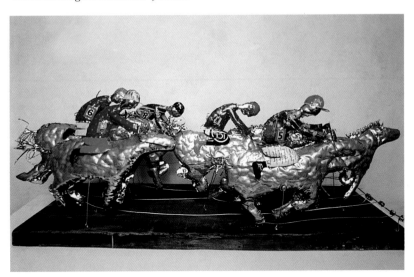

'Horse Race', 1989.

'The Café', 1990

'The Café' was built by Lucy Casson and Andy Hazell for the *Ride of Life*, a 1990 project of automata tableaux in Sheffield's Meadowhall Shopping Centre. Sadly, the project was aborted. Life-sized figures with flip-top heads drank tea, squirted tomato ketchup on their dinner and poured quantities of tea from a huge teapot. It was a frantic scene, with dogs, wobbling food and flies being zapped by a fly zapper. Outside was a street scene of flashing adverts, tower blocks and traffic.

*'The Café' by Lucy
Casson, 1990, with
Andy Hazell.*

Ron Fuller

Born in 1936, Cornishman Ron Fuller studied at Plymouth and Falmouth School of Art and at the Royal College of Art in London, and did his National Service in the Rifle Brigade. He has been interested in toys and models all his life and started a business making them in 1960. The things he makes are usually mechanical and based, mostly, on traditional ideas. His early influence was Sam Smith, then Jack Gould and Yootha Rose and, later, the work of toymakers all over the world, particularly the Germans. Now he is inspired by folk art. As well as toys he makes souvenirs, novelties, automata, games and clocks.

*OPPOSITE PAGE:
'Sheep-Shearing Man' by Ron Fuller, 1985.*

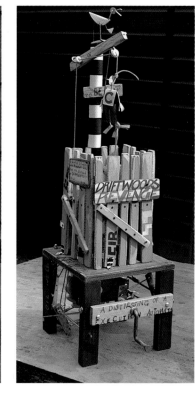

'Tooth Fairy', 1987.　　　　*'Nelson – a Good Man', 1996.*　　　　*'Driftwood Revenge', 1999.*

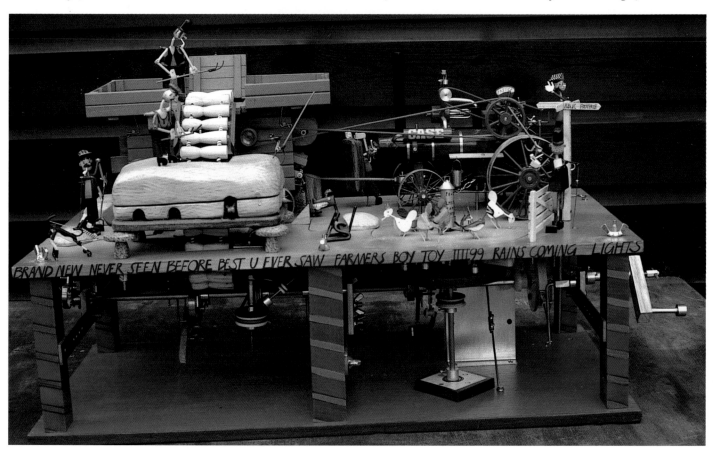

'Threshing Machine' by Ron Fuller, 1999.

John Grayson

John Grayson makes automata from printed tin sheet. He started making mechanical toys while studying three-dimensional design at Wolverhampton University in 1997. The inspiration for his work comes from two sources, his long-time fascination with tinplate toys and a love of making craft objects. Within his toys Grayson juxtaposes the qualities associated with hand-made craft objects with those associated with the industrial mass production of tin toys.

To make his automata he prints coloured imagery on to tin sheet. The printed metal is formed into three-dimensional objects using tabs and slots to hold the components together. By employing these making processes he evokes the qualities associated with Victorian tinplate toys: stylized forms,

bright colours, high lustre, and noisy jerking movements created by simple mechanisms.

Grayson loves the imperfections created in the 'perfect world' of industrial tin-toy manufacture – the missregistration of colours and scuffs caused during printing and assembly. These qualities are reflected in his objects, created through the hand-making process.

Grayson enjoys making objects that echo the world around him, and ships, rockets, spacemen and robots are all typical subject matter for his work. However, his automata are not only a nostalgic echo of the past, but also a response to contemporary things, happenings and events. Often the work is inspired by a narrative, creating a three-dimensional, whimsical and often satirical observation on today's world.

'The Fall and Rise of Reginald', 2000 (470 × 300 × 150mm/18½ × 12 × 6in).

'Go by Bus' by John Grayson, 1998 (450 × 250 × 130mm/18 × 10 × 5in).

ABOVE: '*Gulls*', *1997 (120 × 240 × 120mm/ 4¾ × 9½ × 4¾in).*

ABOVE RIGHT: 'Sparky the Astronaut and Robot', 2000 (90 × 220mm/3½ × 8⅔in).

'*Ewe and I Travel Free*', *1999 (470 × 300 × 150mm/18½ × 12 × 6in).*

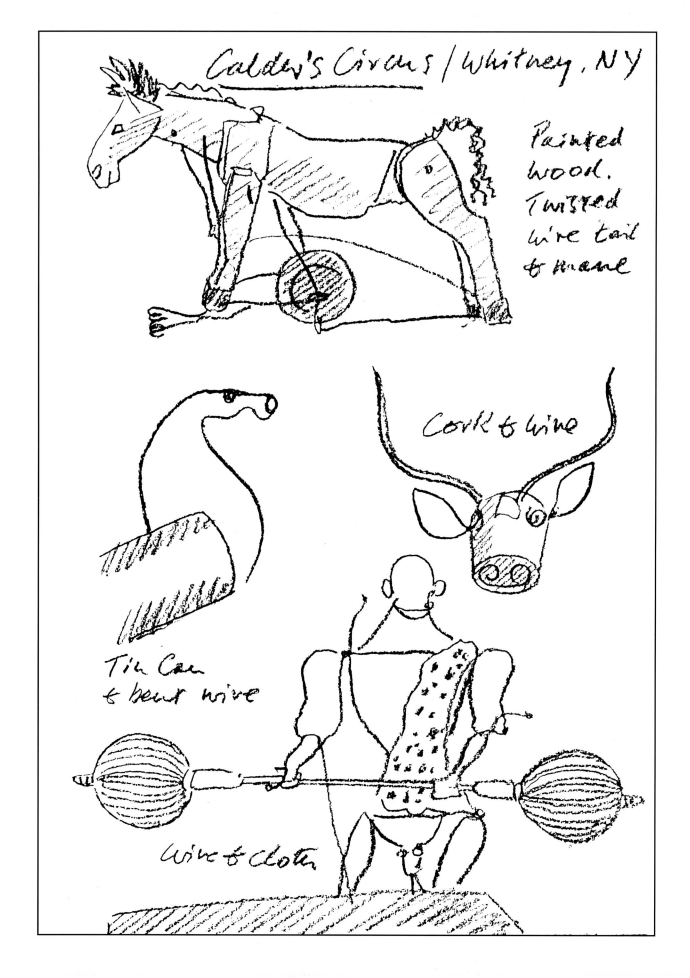

2 THE ORIGINS OF CONTEMPORARY AUTOMATA

Modern automatists owe little to the mechanical maestros who, with the collaboration of expert doll makers, produced luxury automata that graced the drawing rooms of the wealthy in the mid-eighteenth and nineteenth centuries. Their natural successors and beneficiaries were robots, which have revolutionized industry and achieved feats of automation far beyond their legacy.

By contrast, today's automatists are (with a few exceptions, such as Frank Nelson and Paul Spooner) decidedly low-tech. They are content with their modest mechanisms to eschew the intricacies of serious engineering and remote control. It seems to be a common factor that binds most of them, not as a group but as a homogeneous assembly of artist craftsmen and women who want to make things move, but not too efficiently. This is not in any way a reaction against grown-up engineering. Primarily artists, they merely want to infuse a little movement into their art.

There are notable precedents for this in the work of fine artists such as Marcel Duchamp and Alexander Calder, who both experimented in the 1920s and 1930s with motorized sculptures, freeing themselves from the fixed relationships of static composition. Calder rediscovered the spirit of automata making in building his famous miniature wire circus. Although he developed and, indeed, performed it for over thirty years, its influence on automatists has only recently been realized, in the work of such creators as Douglas Wilson.

ALEXANDER CALDER (1898–1976)

Born in Philadelphia, the son of a sculptor, Calder began to build his wire circus in the late 1920s, 'just for the fun of it', because of his love of the circus and making toys. He continued to add figures to his troupe and over the years (eventually filling five suitcases) entertained his friends and fellow artists. As his fame grew, he began to be called upon to give performances at public exhibitions.

In 1961, Carlos Vilardebo directed a colour film entitled *Calder's Circus*, photographed at his home. The film was shown at the Whitney Museum of Art in New York, among other venues, alongside an exhibition of the circus. In the film, Calder manipulates the little wire figures, voicing the ringmaster and introducing the acts in his own gravelly execrable French. His wife, Louisa, plays accompanying gramophone music while Calder himself adds sound effects as the little figures come to life in his hands. They are made mainly of wire, with corks, string, wool, a little wood for plinths and bases, and all kinds of material to serve as cloaks, costumes and floor sheets. The characters are real, with personalities forged in Calder's imagination. He is a child, on his knees, arranging his toys, governing their antics, and providing small scenarios to be enacted by his wire troupe. His enjoyment is infectious and the members of the audience applaud as he opens the show with a hand-cranked horse encircling the ring.

*OPPOSITE PAGE:
Sketches (by Rodney Peppé) based on Alexander Calder's 'Circus', shown at the Whitney Museum of American Art, New York.*

Suddenly, a previously positioned rider springs from the ringside on to the horse's back, drawing more applause and a breathy modest chuckle from Calder.

He then brings on the wild horse, which attempts to buck its rider. A cowboy lassoes a bull, followed by a ballerina with mobile breasts, on springs. She is the target for a demented spear thrower and two stretcher bearers hurry into the ring to carry her off. She returns almost immediately as Calder announces proudly, 'a second ballerina', again with the breathy chuckle to wild applause.

A wonderfully agile kangaroo hops by, seals perform and a belly dancer gyrates to more applause. A wire-framed strongman, cleverly articulated to lift his dumbbell grandly, raises and lowers it carefully, and bows. Fluttering doves descend on to their wasp-waisted trainer followed by Calder's demonstration of his cloth-bound sword swallower with a Dali-esque moustache.

The most colourful (and desirable) piece is the lion in his trailer. Calder takes him from behind the bars, holds him close to his face and emits a frightening roar. He then activates the tamer, who puts his head into the lion's mouth. Frightened by the tamer's pistol, the lion has a domestic accident and Calder carefully covers each dropping, scooping up sawdust with a tiny shovel.

Next come the charioteers driving two horses apiece, brandishing cloth whips, bobbing back and forth as they race each other. The show closes with an aerielist's superb somersault (repeated) and a dive through a paper hoop, as we hear again that little modest breathy chuckle of Calder's.

As the film ends with Calder walking away from camera down a sunlit, tree-lined path towards his home, the watcher feels privileged to have witnessed, albeit in capsule form, a unique event in the evolution of modern automata. When asked about his interest in the circus, Calder said, 'I love the mechanics of the thing – and the vast space – and the spotlight'.

JEAN TINGUELY (1925–91)

Born in Fribourg, Switzerland, Jean Tinguely, like Duchamp and Calder, wanted to make his constructivist forms move. Although Tinguely was very active in the 1950s, it was not until London's Tate Gallery mounted a memorable retrospective of his work, in 1982, that he became more widely known in Britain.

Tinguely's noisy machines, some of them monumental, created images of digested and disgorged footballs, crushed bottles and plates, and self-painted *meta mechanica* abstract pictures. He also made sculptures to self-destruct, notably his *Homage to New York* (1960), which had to be extinguished by the New York Fire Department in the garden of the city's Museum of Modern Art, much to the chagrin of the invited patrons.

Tinguely's ironic comments on human and mechanical behaviour have left their mark on some of today's automatists, in much the same way as Tinguely himself was influenced by his Dada forbears. He revelled in ambiguity. He was a kinetic artist who mocked kineticism, or at least the sort that revered technology, and it is this kind of paradox that appeals to modern makers of automata.

SAM SMITH (1908–83)

The seminal figure of Sam Smith looms large in the provenance of modern automata. His considerable influence on two generations of automatists is indisputable; indeed, it is clear from some of the statements by the makers in this book. Not one major exhibition catalogue of the genre fails to mention this remarkably original artist, and the debt that modern automatists owe to him. Although not strictly an automatist himself, making only limited jointed movements held by string, and simple jumping jack mechanisms, Smith admired and encouraged certain automatists, and

'NEWS' by Sam Smith, 1976. 'The story so far: The horse-riding semaphorist has to get the NEWS over the lake:
he takes a boat.' The piece is 381mm (15in) long.

*'The General', a jumping
jack by Sam Smith, 1976.
Gouache on paper, design
for painted wood with
collage, feathers, etc.
The sketch measures
340 × 235mm
(13¾ × 9¼in).*

also helped others whom he had never met. It had the effect of laying a matrix for future development which continues to this day.

Born in Southampton, the son of a cross-Channel ferry captain, Sam Smith studied painting in Bournemouth and at the Westminster School of Art in London. It was here that he met Gladys, his future wife, who was to play such a supportive role in his later career. Although he picked up the rudiments of drawing, he learned nothing about techniques, nor was he stuffed with theories. He was glad of this; he came to believe that too much of either could stifle creativity. Before the Second World War he was encouraged by Muriel Rose to exhibit carvings at her Little Gallery in London's Sloane Street. Although he had aspirations to become a painter, he soon realized, as he said towards the end of his life, that an artist must find a language which is natural to him; his language was wood.

During the war he designed Bailey Bridges, which instilled an orderliness in his work that persisted throughout his career. After the war he became a graphic artist and developed a passion for making marionettes and other wooden objects. At first they were about loneliness but the themes later changed, to attempt to discover what people were like behind their masks. By the mid-1950s he had adopted a boat theme that was to last the rest of his life. The boats themselves assumed just as much personality as their mismatched occupants.

In the mid-1960s, Smith's work was shown at Primavera and the Portal Gallery, both in London. His pieces seemed to strike a chord with the American sense of humour and folk art tradition, and were exhibited in New York and Boston and on the west coast of the USA. By the 1970s, he was firmly established selling his work quickly to collectors in the USA, especially in California, and his work also began to reach a wider public in Britain. In 1972 he had a major exhibition at the Bristol City Art Gallery, which toured to Beaford Arts Centre in Devon and the Camden Arts Centre in London. The exhibition was critically acclaimed and Edward Lucie-Smith included Smith in his book *Art in the Seventies* (Phaidon Press, 1980). 'The veteran Sam Smith', he wrote, 'was almost invariably until recently described as a "toymaker", and was included in craft shows rather than exhibitions. If these are toys, they are remarkably sophisticated ones, with a freight of complex meaning.'

Preliminary sketch for 'NEWS' by Sam Smith.

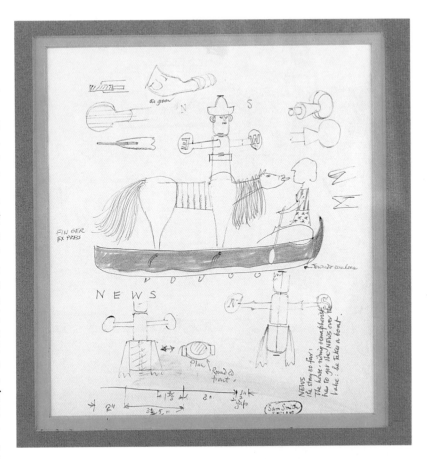

Part of that 'freight' was described by the artist in exhibition catalogues towards the end of his career: 'As I get older, I get less interested in the way a thing looks and more interested in the spirit that hides within it: so the things I make are meant to be looked into, rather than looked at.'

Sam Smith's fame was given another important boost with the Arts Council of Great Britain's award-winning film, *Sam Smith: Genuine England*, directed by Dudley Shaw Ashton and first transmitted by the BBC in 1976. The film's title, which refers to the legend written on all his pieces, is explained by the artist as follows: 'Since I found my things were copied they all carry a written guarantee that I did them and they're British.' In the film, Smith shares the screen with his pieces, contributing a number of insights: 'To me, eyes are not a way of looking out, but a way of looking in.' And on his method of working: 'When I'm working I have an idea and I work the idea out. And I might make half a dozen things related to that idea – and that's finished. It's gone for ever, because I'm working on something else.'

His own role is characteristically modest: 'My life was something like a magic lantern. The scene flickers for a moment and then goes for ever, leaving only a myth. I make the myths into people – well, I don't really make them – they make themselves,' he says, adding, 'I'm just here to watch and give a hand occasionally.'

Smith loved words, and would play with them and write them on his objects. 'The Story So Far...' would preface the legends to many pieces. For example, 'The horse-

Packing box for 'NEWS' by Sam Smith, 1976. Gouache on strawboard (407 × 356 × 133mm/16 × 14 × 5¼in).

'Entrance Grand Pier, Weston-Super-Mare, 1904'. Sam Smith, pen and ink (102 × 102mm/ 4 × 4in).

riding semaphorist has to get the NEWS over the lake: he takes a boat.' But the observer is getting only half the story; the rest is in the artist's head. In the case of 'NEWS' (in the author's collection; *see* the photo on page 31), the other half is printed in the Serpentine Gallery Catalogue caption: 'The Messenger is fortunate,' it reads. 'He hires a boat which belongs to a girl who looks very like Miss America 1924. He's in the whirligig tradition of American folk art. NEWS is an important word because it brings in the four points of the compass.'

Another boat piece in the author's collection, made in 1973, reads: 'The Story So Far: Frederick is convinced he has not married Angela for her money, or because her father is a life peer.' As in the case of 'NEWS', a wonderful fish decorates the bottom of the boat. In another boat piece, a beautiful, solemn-looking mermaid with a voluptuous torso comes as a salty surprise on the bottom of the boat.

Sam Smith's references were based on childhood memories of the music hall, the fairground, the circus, the cinema and, above all, the sea and his beloved boats. Within these themes he wove his own mythology and observations of the human psyche. Storytelling played a strong part in the making of his pieces, so it is not surprising that he subsequently produced two children's books, for Timothy Benn of the publisher Ernest Benn Ltd; *The Secret Harbour* (1975) was followed in 1977 by *Rover's Regatta Day*.

In the following letter, dated 30 January 1977, Sam Smith refers to the film *Sam Smith: Genuine England* and his reaction to it; the puppets he designed for an animated display commissioned by Pentagram for Riverdale Shopping Centre, Lewisham, London; and his venture into the author's world of children's books.

Dear Rodney
It was nice of you to send those pictures with your letter. We saw the film in a cinema, and the shock of seeing myself oversize was so great I could only begin to see it when I was not present and just the things filled the screen: I thought the last minute or so, when the things were outside in the garden, were magical: that was the part I enjoyed.

The puppets I designed about three years ago for the new shopping centre at Lewisham are now working. At last! It was almost too much for Gladys, who dropped a tear when they appeared for the first time. Some of them I had not seen completed, so it was mostly fresh to me: but I was pleased, the movements and timing were just as I had planned. It was all over very quickly, so we sat around in the air-conditioned comfort and waited for the next show, one hour later: they come out every hour. The lighting on the figures is not too good. There was talk two years ago of spots but all that must have been economized out in the interval without anyone telling me. In fact we only heard the puppets were working when a girl we know, who had gone shopping in Sainsbury's, wrote to tell us. Do have a look if you are ever in the Lewisham area. I should like to know your opinion, and whether you think they could ever be photographed? The only records I have are some pictures of the scale models.

Good of you to go to the exhibition. It was a last-minute thought on someone's part to borrow as many of the pieces used in the film as possible. I am just coming to the end of another children's book, which has taken an unbelievably long time – four months in fact. But I wanted to avoid all the errors and every word and full stop has been worried over. Now I am near the end it's all flowing out quite easily; which is what often happens to me. When the book is away, I shall start on a project with a London gallery; and then I want to make a figure to go outside a new store in Seattle; and all the time there is a race against the clock to try to make things for people who have been waiting ages for something of mine: I'm 68, and some of them are more! With all the shopping centre jobs and so on, I have little time to make things and so literally the only ones I have are WHO AM I?, NEWS and the BIRDFEEDERS. I must keep these because there are always the occasions when I feel compelled to lend a piece to a worthy exhibition. I was going to lend them to the Ulster Museum, but I think they got the impression I was nutty as I said I was opposed to biographical details of artists in catalogues, on the grounds that what someone did ten years ago has no relevance to what he does now. Anyhow, when I also said I was against cameras, and never had my things photographed, it was too much; they never came to collect! I became anti-camera because we had been on a holiday trip, and I found that Scandinavians, Germans, Dutch, but mainly Japanese, used cameras as stand-ins for eyes, and made no effort to see anything but let the camera do it for them: there was a man on a bus who set his camera with some sort of time control to take a picture from the window, to the frame of which it was firmly clamped, every few minutes, while he went to sleep and snored until we reached the town. Now of course, I am feeling camera kinder...

One of these days, who knows, we may make a grand trip and call on you... I do want

to get to Kent to see a puppet theatre that has been decorated by my friend Fred, with whom I worked on the Lewisham project: he is the last and grandest of the fairground artists...

Sam & Gladys

Sadly, the puppet show has been dismantled. Unfortunately, the cost of mechanical maintenance made the puppets unviable and they disappeared some years ago.

Sam Smith was generous with advice to devotees who wrote to him, telephoned or visited him. This generosity even spread to giving presents of his small pieces to the author's young children on his and his wife's first visit to Sam Smith and Gladys at Kingswear in Devon.

Frank Nelson described Sam Smith as the nicest man he had ever met. Peter Markey says that he learned from Frank Nelson that Sam Smith liked his (Peter's) work because it was recognizable as his. He was always cross about blatant plagiarism especially as there was a thriving industry in Sam Smith copies. When Frank Nelson showed his work to Sam Smith, Smith apparently said that this was the sort of work he always wanted to do, but that he did not have the expertise.

Another of Sam Smith's letters, this one dated 3 July 1980, extols the talents of these two leading automatists.

Dear Rodney
It was good to see Tatjana and Jonathan on Sunday... I hope Tatjana managed to find Peter Markey in Falmouth. He is doing some really outstanding things with movements – sometimes simple, sometimes as complex as a fugue – mainly based on variations on the theme of a cam. He is very original and has a vigorous and joyful style which I find quite compelling. Frank Nelson went to see him but I have not heard yet how they got along.

Frank's intuitive knowledge of mechanical movement is impressive. He can use mechanics as an ingredient of art and has marvellous ideas about programming his pieces, as in a silver wedding gift he was commissioned to make for an optician. This looked like a traditional optician's sign, a large pair of specs, but when you touched a lever the lenses fell out of the specs and revealed profile portraits of the optician and his lady, very well done in relief, which, on a further touch of the control, moved forward and out of the spectacle frame and very beautifully kissed. I think Frank's work in the future will increasingly be with commissions of this nature: he has a special genius for that sort of thing and a very real humanity. Recently he worked for a week with the students at Parnham. I saw the things before they were finished and was really thrilled by the imaginative results he got from earnest young people who had never had anything to do with anything so lighthearted before…

So it's back to work shortly, back to a rather evil hominoid white-headed eagle I am making, who somehow stands for the westward trek of the whites towards the Rockies…

During my engineering war years, when I was Bailey Bridging, every detail drawn had a name and a number and then on the assembly drawing each piece was arrowed. This way anyone could see where all the bits went, otherwise the war would have gone on for years while sappers tried to find out what fitted where. On to something different – recently I saw in a house some very beautiful Indian toys. These appeared to be made of rather blackish clay which had been fired and decorated with small threadlike extrusions of what looked like coloured wax, which made the decoration on the costume, the hair, features and so on. The arms revolved on an L-shaped wire. Have you ever seen anything like this and do you know what part of India it would come from? I'd never seen anything like it.

Well – time I got back to me eagle. But more about the book. Contrary to your instruction, I read the gobbledygook. I just could not understand the Monkey. So I made it out of paper and found it worked very well. Good show. I am not sure your way is the only way though. I seem to remember I had a Victorian book of the

Like v. miniature cake icing

'Things Every Good Boy Can Make For His Sister' kind which had a different system. But I have not seen it in years and cannot find it so I may be up a gum tree…

How long will your show be at the Bethnal Green? I should get to town for a rush around shortly. Are you sure you want a machine? It really depends whether you want to make individual pieces or be a ✦✦✦✦ production runner. I now have no machine except for a drill, and like the results better.

All best wishes
Congratulations and Love to All

Sam

From 5 December 1980 to 8 February 1981, the Serpentine Gallery in London's Hyde Park held a major retrospective of Sam Smith's work. Sadly, he was unable to attend due to illness, which prevented him from working at all. It was the cruellest of ironies that an artist who was actually improving with age should be cut down by a severe stroke. It not only robbed him of speech but of the ability to write and even form letters.

It was almost as if he had foreseen the tragedy, for Harpies had re-entered his work with a vengeance. Dark as they were, however, the last masterpieces he made, 'NUNC' and 'Unaware New York 18 May 22', illuminated the end of his career. In describing them for the Serpentine Gallery exhibition catalogue, he wrote, 'There is a Harpy on my shoulder as I write.'

Impossible to categorize, Sam Smith's pieces were neither toys nor sculpture but something in between, which the world of fine art could not accept because it could not define them. They were toys, but toys for *his* imagination.

If there are words to sum up this remarkable artist they are perhaps to be found in the opening of his film: 'Children's toys', he says, 'are mainly about pretending to be grown up. The things I make are about what it's like when you get there.'

CABARET MECHANICAL THEATRE

Sam Smith may be difficult to categorize, but Cabaret Mechanical Theatre (or CMT, as it has become known) falls neatly into the automata and mechanical toys slot. Its creator and founder Sue Jackson, a former Falmouth art student, can fairly lay claim to have put the genre, in its modern form, on the map.

In 1979, Sue Jackson opened a crafts shop called 'Cabaret' in Falmouth, Cornwall. She founded CMT in 1983, before moving to London's Covent Garden in 1985, turning the former vegetable vaults into a cavernous hybrid between a gallery, a museum and a shop. The site housed the first and only collection of contemporary automata in Britain, made by artists originally recruited in Falmouth.

For the next fifteen years, always on a financial knife edge, but crowded with tourists and enthusiasts, Sue Jackson managed the business of CMT successfully. Eventually, however, the £100,000-a-year running costs forced a move to Southend-on-Sea. At the time of writing, the future of CMT is a secret.

With its core of Britain's finest automatists, CMT has been the flagship for two decades in an ever-growing ocean of activity in automata making. In the beginning, the wooden, hand-cranked Wave Machines by Peter Markey, her first recruit, were followed by the work of Paul Spooner whose first piece of automata depicted Anubis, the Egyptian jackal (god of the dead) drawing a sausage. Toymaker Ron Fuller was attracted to CMT too, and it wasn't long before Sue Jackson had them all making coin-in-the-slot machines, to finance themselves and CMT. With the move to London, other makers joined. Tim Hunkin, Lucy Casson and Andy Hazell were followed in due course by Jan Zalud and Keith Newstead. Newstead's video *How to Make Automata*, directed by Gary Alexander, was

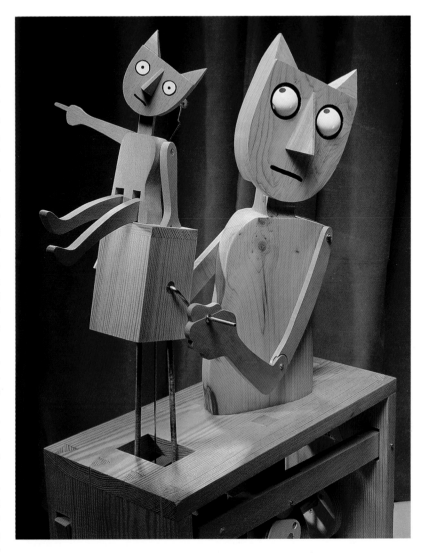

marketed by CMT. Other videos included *Cabaret Mechanical Video*, a catalogue of the collection, with artist interviews, and *Made in Stithians*, an amusing and inspiring portrait of Paul Spooner at work.

The first-time visitor to CMT was riveted by an astonishing sight – Paul Spooner's masterpiece, 'Last Judgement', a 112cm (45in) moving skeleton based on a Hieronymous Bosch painting. Impressed by this first piece, visitors were never disappointed as they proceeded inside. The shop sold affordable automata and cheaply priced paper and wooden kits, while the

'Barecats', by Paul Spooner and Matt Smith. The name of the symbol of Cabaret Mechanical Theatre's 'Barecat', is an anagram of 'Cabaret'.

Cabaret Mechanical Theatre, Covent Garden – the shop area.

exhibition area, guarded by an automaton ticket inspector who stamped tickets, was packed with machines that responded to the touch of a button or thrust of a coin. It was cavernous and excitingly lit, entrancing children and adults, collectors and fellow automatists.

For the first time, CMT provided a place where automata were presented in a friendly, confident environment, reminiscent of the old end-of-the-pier arcades, but without any of their sad tattiness. Something else was new – a slightly off-centre way of looking at the world. It was something between idiosyncracy and anarchy, with an underlying sense of fun and the absurd. There were witty ideas everywhere.

At the end of the 1980s, Sue Jackson was approached by the design director of the Meadowhall Shopping Centre in Sheffield to expand, on a huge scale, what she had created at CMT. She was asked to think of a theme to fill 1,395m² (15,000sq ft) in the fast-food area, to attract customers. A completely free hand was given, together with a retainer to cover research, which included a visit to Disneyland by CMT's Paul Spooner, Tim Hunkin and Gary Alexander. While they admired the excellence of the engineering and the execution,

the CMT group agreed that the blandness common to most theme parks was to be avoided. Their theme for Meadowhall developed as a satire on the British way of life. Contributions came from dozens of makers, all with different styles and personalities, from all over the country, and the *Ride of Life* was conceived.

Tragically, the *Ride of Life* never saw the light of day. At a fairly advanced stage, the project was ended. The men in suits did pay for the completion of the twenty sets, which were eventually stored in cardboard boxes in Rotherham, never to be used for the purpose for which they were designed. What started as a wonderful dream in the booming 1980s had a very rude awakening with the recession of the 1990s. The scale of the project had excited Sue Jackson from the outset and seeing all that creativity and production time condemned to cardboard boxes was a heartbreaking disappointment. Paul Spooner felt numbed, but somewhat relieved. Tim Hunkin thought a great opportunity for fruitful collaboration had been missed and Andy Hazell suggested that the project should go to Japan. In his opinion, Britain didn't deserve it.

What could and should have been a landmark in the history of automata was abandoned because of a simple commercial decision. In ten years, no organization has installed the *Ride* elsewhere and the chance for shoppers to see themselves portrayed in a satirical, albeit friendly manner has been lost. Generations of automatists were deprived of a wonderful opportunity, too. The project was probably the closest automatists have ever come to forming a group and, while this is not necessarily desirable, it is interesting to consider how it might have developed had the *Ride* succeeded. Certainly, the automatists at CMT, although closely knit, have never become a group, beyond working under the auspices of Sue Jackson.

Sue Jackson has played a pivotal role, not only in the development of CMT but also in terms of influencing the making of contemporary automata in Britain. This has been done mainly with travelling exhibitions and the publication of *CMT News*. Both provide a continual source of mechanical reference for enthusiasts, collectors and students.

Four days before CMT closed in London, an article by Martin Plimmer appeared in the *Evening Standard* for 8 March 2000, under the headline 'Farewell to the Enchanted Cabaret'. He described it as a 'tiny, crowded, unsubsidized and obstinately and enchantingly British. No other place so evocatively sums up British ingenuity, creativity, nostalgia, irreverence, idiosyncracy and sense of humour.' He goes on to describe the machines as 'part theatre, part junk sculpture, part toy and part joke. They mimic human behaviour in a way which is uniquely absurd and revealing.'

CMT's presence in London will be missed as a tourist attraction, but the real loss will be felt by those who regularly visited the premises in order to 'service' their mechanical aesthetics. Whatever form CMT takes in the future its part in the development of modern automata has already left an indelible mark. Sue Jackson's contribution in taking up the threads sewn by Calder, Tinguely and especially Sam Smith cannot be overestimated.

On 14 February 2002 a press release appeared with the headline: 'British Mechanical Toy Museum merges with Hollywood entertainment Company'. The Valentine's Day announcement reported that CMT and Scenery West, a leading Hollywood entertainment construction company, are in the process of restoring the automata collection and re-creating Cabaret in Los Angeles, under the new company name, IRDM (It Really Doesn't Matter).

The contact addresses are:

Tim Knipe at IRDM,
11461 Hart St., North Hollywood,
CA 91605.
Phone: 818 765 8661
email: tknipe@scenerywest.com

In Europe, contact:

Sarah Alexander at IRDM,
Unit 15, 95 Wilton Road,
London SW1V 1BZ.
Phone: +44 (0) 208 516 3134
email: sarah@cabaret.co.uk

Cabaret Mechanical Theatre frontage and courtyard.

MAKERS' WORK

Neil Hardy

I have been designing and making automata for the last eight years and feel I have only just started to understand how some of my pieces really work. As I tend to make a lot of repeats of the same thing, I am gradually finding every possible way in which a piece can go wrong and so beginning to learn what makes them really tick. It also means I can refine and adjust the mechanism over time until it is fairly foolproof. I enjoy finding the right mechanism for each piece so that it fits the movements in a unique way and like to show the levers and cams and bits of wire so that everyone can work out how turning a handle at one end can create various movements at the other.

Neil Hardy's pieces range from the simplest – two shy tortoises sticking their heads out for a furtive kiss – to the more fiddly and awkward to make, the anteater and the early bird (*see* photos on pages 41–2). The anteater has a long tongue that gradually slides down into the ant nest and then returns, while ants scurry back and forth. Making something move in a straight line, for a long distance, is one of the most difficult challenges and getting the anteater's tongue to move the whole length of the piece required some interesting pulley systems, more commonly found on cranes than on anteaters. 'The Early Bird' shows Eddy pulling a worm as his two bird mates gossip in the background. After a while the lower door opens, revealing the worm to be the tail of a large carnivore, which eventually rises to catch the bird. The problem with this piece is that, apart from getting all the mechanisms in below, Hardy also had to hide the carnivore, and try and keep him as a surprise.

'The Bat' and 'The Penguins' show how some simple movements from the animals can tell a complete story. The monochrome penguin mother looks on in shock as her newly hatched son reveals himself to be a multicoloured genetic freak. She leans forwards in horror before keeling over backwards in a dead coma. The vampire bat shows how frightening these creatures were before they developed fangs. Opening its wings dramatically, it sticks out its tongue to scare away predators.

For thirteen years, until 1992, I had been working in London, Cambridge and Edinburgh as an architect. During this period I became more and more interested in mechanical models and how they worked. As a child I had always been intrigued by the works and drawings of Heath Robinson and Emett and I began to make simple models based on their particular style and humour.

In about 1988 I came across the Cabaret Mechanical Theatre in Covent Garden, where some of the finest automata are on exhibition. The humour, craftsmanship and mechanical design of the work intrigued and fascinated me. Noticing that the public were actually prepared to buy some of the pieces, it began to dawn on me that it might be possible to earn a living from this craft. In November 1992 I decided to pursue this hobby full time and started in earnest designing and creating new automata.

Since that time I have found a number of craft shops and galleries who have sold my work on a regular basis throughout the UK. In 1994/5 I began to receive letters from abroad enquiring about the pieces and they are now being sold in a number of galleries from Paris to Tokyo as well as in the USA.

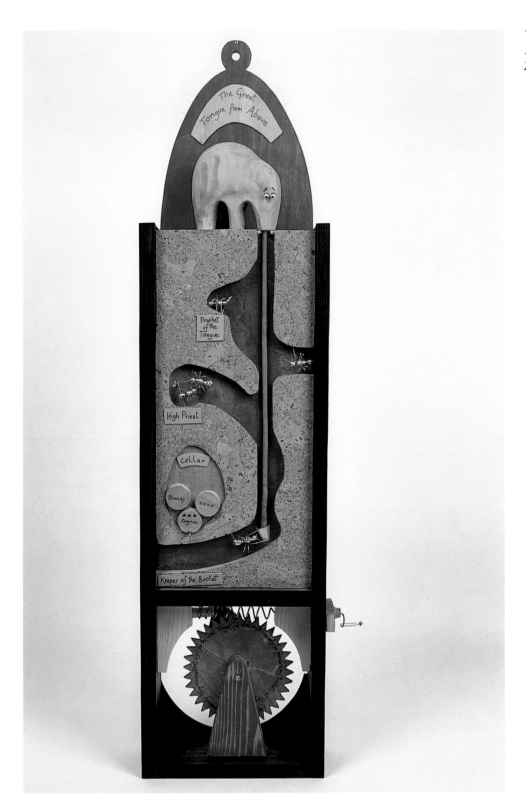

'Anteater' by Neil Hardy,
1997 (661 × 165 × 76mm/
26 × 6½ × 3in).

'Early Bird' (175 × 60 × 60mm/7 × 2¼ × 2¼in).

'Bat', 1996 (229 × 178 × 76mm/9 × 7 × 3in).

LEFT: 'Penguins', 1993 (152 × 254 × 102mm/6 × 10 × 4in).

ABOVE: 'Tortoise', 1995 (130 × 120 × 70mm/5 × 4¾ × 2¾in).

Andy Hazell

I came to working in tinplate through my association with Lucy Casson. Together, we progressed from crude bobbly tin, wire and solder assemblages that outraged the readers of Crafts magazine, to marginally less crude, less wobbly stuff. Over the years, biscuit tins became disguised and motor oil came in plastic containers. Tin remains a wonderfully quick, malleable medium, even if sometimes it's like working with a big unfriendly razor blade.

The simplest crank motion still enthralls the computer generation for probably the same length of time as a cheap game – I guess around 20 seconds.

I create little movements in time – film stills. I imagine what a person does, eats, thinks. I build a whole scenario around that individual.

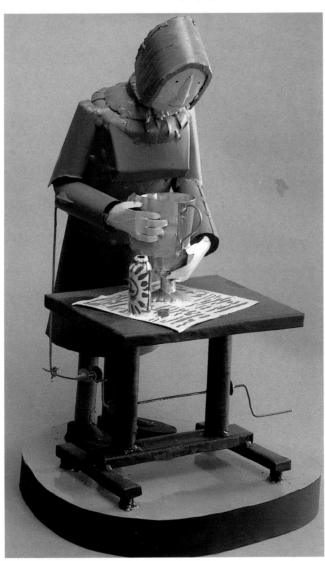

'The Bowling Trophy', 1996 (300mm/12in high).

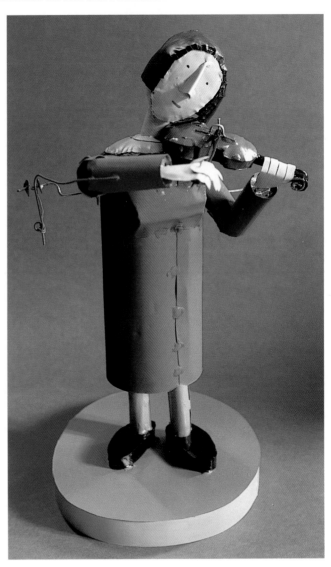

'The Violinist', 1996 (300mm/12in high).

'Big Fish' by Andy Hazell, 1995 (300mm/12in high).

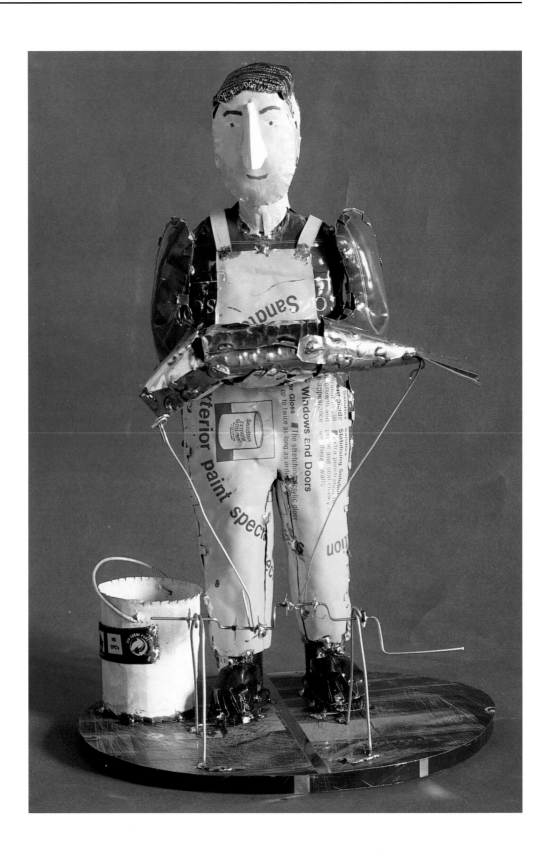

'Wash 'n' Go', 1995
(300mm/12in long).

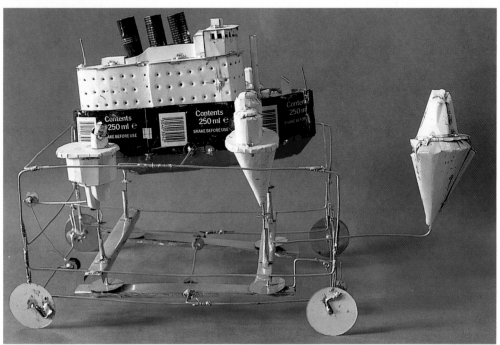

'Titanic', 1996
(300mm/12in long).

Tim Hunkin

Trained in engineering science at Cambridge, Tim Hunkin drew a cartoon for a student magazine which led to a weekly strip for the *Observer*, 'The Rudiments of Wisdom'. This became popular and ran for fourteen years. His successful television series, *The Secret Life of Machines*, drew upon his expertise with domestic machines, which themselves provided mechanical sources for his work as an automatist.

'The General', 1985
The spectator places the missile in the General's hand. He then slowly rotates, soaring and diving the missile like a child with a toy plane. He finally drops the missile in the litter bin.

Disgusted with the world of fine art, I started making things for charities. I made this for the local women's peace group to make their market stall look less drab.

'The Zoo', 1980
The idea is that the spectator is the animal in the cage. On inserting a coin, the mother throws peanuts through the bars while the child jumps manically about and finally squirts the spectator with his water pistol. The father just rolls his head looking bemused.

I made mechanical contraptions as a child, but stopped during my teens, thinking it was childish. 'The Zoo' was one of the first pieces I made when I returned to making things in my late twenties.

'The Chiropodist', 1987
The spectator is instructed to remove their shoe and place their foot in the hole in the bottom of the machine. The chiropodist looks down, rubs her fingers in a slightly menacing way, and then drops down beneath her counter (triggering strange things to rub across the foot).

'The Chiropodist' was made for Cabaret Mechanical Theatre in Covent Garden, London. This was so full of tourists that, at its peak, the machine took nearly £20,000 in 20p pieces in a year – very satisfying.

'The Anthropologists' Fund Raising Ritual', 1997
As a visitor approaches, the anthropologists rise up and point accusingly (with their eyes glowing, almost as if in a trance). When a coin is inserted they bend over (originally intended as a bow of thanks, but actually looks more as if they are simply inspecting the donation).

I like making collecting boxes. As with all coin-operated automata, spectators are paying to be entertained (rather than to own the piece). Having parted with cash, they invariably pay considerable attention, and never wander off. Collecting boxes have the added attraction that they get placed in interesting prominent positions. In the case of the Pitt Rivers where this piece is kept, the museum also has a particularly rich collection, which I found very inspiring.

'The Builder and his Wife', 1982
The builder scratches his head and then his wife shrugs her shoulders. They were part of a whole exhibition of 'spectators' at an art gallery, all viewed through empty picture frames.

After an earlier exhibition at the ICA in London, I had become disillusioned with the pretentiousness and hype of the world of fine art. Making the spectators was therapeutic to some extent, but I have never been tempted to have an art gallery exhibition ever again.

'The General' by Tim Hunkin, 1985.

'The Zoo', 1980.

RIGHT: 'The Chiropodist', 1987.

LEFT:
'The Anthropologists'
Fund Raising Ritual',
1997.

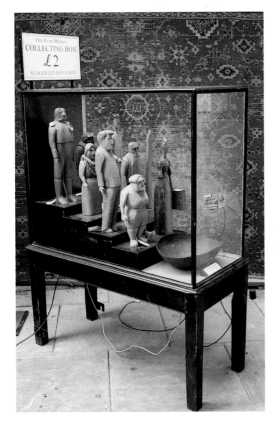

'The Builder and his Wife', 1982.

3 TOOLS AND MATERIALS

TOOLS

Choosing tools is a personal thing, like filling up a shopping basket. The following is a list of woodworking tools, with brief descriptions. Specialist tools for carving and turning are not included, neither are metalworking tools, other than files and rasps. Clearly you cannot, and would not wish to, buy everything on the list, but, with a knowledge of what is available, you can decide what to put in your particular basket.

A **woodworking bench** is expensive to buy new, so make your own from plans featured in DIY books and magazines. A rough guide for size is 838mm high × 1,525mm long × 610mm deep (33 × 60 × 24in). It must be rigidly built in hardwood (such as beech) with bolts, and the top should be at least 50mm (2in) thick.

A **Workmate** is a small portable bench, which folds up for storage and provides an adaptable work surface at two levels: one standard, and the other for sawing wood. The whole surface is a giant vice with adjusting handles operating an opening of 100mm (4in).

The **power drill** is the most versatile of all power tools because, with its numerous accessories and attachments, it can mimic the actions of other specialist tools. Choose one with a variable speed and a 13mm (½in) chuck.

Drill stands are available in vertical and horizontal versions and must be compatible with your particular drill. Used horizontally, the drill can partially convert into a lathe. This accessory is not as accurate as the more solidly constructed **pillar drill** or **drill press**, which has a heavy base and sturdily built-in power drill.

Drill bits are sold in imperial and metric measurements. To give yourself the widest selection, buy a set of each, starting at 1mm to 10mm (nineteen bits) and the imperial equivalent. For larger sizes you will need a set of six flat auger bits starting at 10mm going up to 25mm and the imperial equivalent; although it must be said that the alternative scale is not so important at the larger sizes.

The **woodworker's vice** holds timber while it is worked. It attaches to the underside of the bench at the front, near the leg. The movable jaw is operated by a handle, which turns a screw running the length of the vice.

A **clamp-on machinist's vice** is lightweight and clamps on to the woodwork bench edge.

A **wooden handscrew** grips both parallel and tapering work with a wide gripping area but does not have the strength of a G-clamp.

A **powered jigsaw** has blades for coarse and fine cutting as well as for cutting curves in wood. It is ideal for heavier-duty work, cutting up to 25mm (1in) thick. Its other advantage is that it does not have the restrictive throat of the fret or scroll saw.

The **powered circular saw** can be an attachment to a power drill or, more effectively, a self-contained power saw. It cuts straight lines in timber up to 38mm (1½in) thick. It must be fitted with an upper and lower blade guard for safety. Children must be kept away from this power tool because of its continuing rotary action when switched off. The main blades you need are rip, cross-cut and combination.

A **hand saw** is used to cut large planks or panels, while a **rip saw** cuts along the length of the grain. A **cross-cut saw** cuts against the grain, scoring two lines and removing the waste between. The **panel saw** is a smaller version of the cross-cut saw, and is useful for cutting plywood panels. A **tenon saw** is used for accurate work such as cutting dovetails. It has a straight, rigid blade parallel to a heavy ridge along the back. A **coping saw** is used to make curved cuts in wood. It has a very narrow blade fitting into a 'U'-shaped frame held under tension by the spring of the frame. A **fretsaw** cuts tight curves in wood and has an even thinner blade than the coping saw and a much deeper throat. A **pad saw** cuts holes in wood with a long thin blade. It is a hand-tool version of the powered jigsaw. The **hole saw** has a drill bit centred within a pressed steel cup and backing plate, which accommodates circular saw blades of various sizes within its concentric ridges. This attachment fits into the drill chuck. The **hacksaw** is used mainly for cutting metal. The **junior hacksaw** is better in confined spaces. The blade has 32 teeth per 25mm (1in) and is held under tension by the frame.

The **powered fretsaw** or **scroll saw** is the best light-duty machine for making small, tightly curved cuts in wood up to 19mm (¾in) thick. You can operate the machine, feeding through the work, within a 280mm (11in) throat, with both hands. The Aeropiccola 71 Vibro Saw, an Italian model that may still be available, is highly recommended because, since the blade vibrates, it does not cut fingers. The **bench jigsaw** is a heavier-duty version of the above, cutting up to 50mm (2in) thickness in wood. This is not an alternative: you really need both machines in order to accommodate light and heavier work. The throat of this machine is about 380mm (15in). It is unsafe for children.

A **mitre box** is a hand-operated metal device, which guides the saw in cutting accurate mitre and right-angle joints. Cheap wooden (beech) ones are sold, as are mitre saws.

Using a **steel rule** with imperial and metric calibrations incised into the metal ensures that there is no slippage of dividers when measuring. A **flexible rule** allows you measure up to 3m (10ft); a spring-loaded mechanism ensures instant return on release. Some have a lock to hold the extended tape and a useful hook on the end to anchor it.

The **G-clamp** (or **cramp**) has a flexible shoe fitted to a ball on the end of the screw, and a sliding Tommy bar at the top. Scrap blocks should be used to protect the work from bruising. Long-reach versions, with deep throats, are made to hold the work some distance from the edge. A **spring clamp** provides light pressure when glueing. It is quickly and easily applied to the work.

Screwdrivers come in all shapes and sizes, but you will need two basic types of tip: the **flared tip**, which is slotted, and the cross-headed types, Phillips and Pozidrive. There are a number of different screw heads available, so it is essential to make sure that they fit your screwdriver. A **cabinet screwdriver** drives slotted screws. An **electrician's screwdriver** has a thin shaft to drive machine screws in electrical plugs and small screws in wood and metal. A **stubby screwdriver** drives screws in restricted places. A **ratchet screwdriver** allows you to drive screws without having to alter your grip. A thumb slide adjusts the action, clockwise, anticlockwise and in fixed position. An **offset screwdriver** drives screws in inaccessible places. A **jeweller's screwdriver set** can be used to drive in miniature screws. **Power screwdriver bits** drive screws with a variable-speed drill.

A **claw hammer** is used for general carpentry and for extracting nails. A **cross pein hammer** has a tapered pein, which enables you to tap in a nail between the fingers to start it off. A **pin hammer** is used to drive in panel pins or tacks.

The **power belt sander** runs on a continuous abrasive belt around two rollers. Choose a model with a dust bag and extractor, and one which has a bench attachment, so that it can be used with the belt upwards. The rollers are adjustable for tension and tracking of the belt. The machine is not cheap and is highly dangerous to fingers where the abrasive moves under the metal. Children must not be allowed near it. It is also possible to buy a **power sanding disc** as an attachment for an electric drill, made of rubber with a steel shank. It will leave cross-grain scratches, but is excellent for removing surface wood. The **foam drum sander** is an attachment for sanding flat and curved surfaces. It has a continuous abrasive belt fitted round a foam drum with a central shaft to fit in the chuck of your drill. An **abrasive flapwheel** is made up of a series of abrasive flaps centred on a shaft. It gives a greater flexibility to the sanding of shapes than the drum sander, but it may be difficult to obtain. The **powered orbital sander** smooths a surface to a final finish or reduces it with a coarse abrasive. A strip of abrasive paper is locked around a rubber pad to give high-speed orbital cuts. Attachments are sold for electric drills. Beware of placing the orbital sander in a vice, as the orbital shaking action does much to reduce its life span. For a fixed position a belt sander should be used, with bench supports.

Files and **rasps** should never be used without their handles because the tang (the bit that goes into the handle) is dangerously narrow. Despite this, few files are sold with handles! They tend to be sold separately. Here are some to choose from:

◆ flat file to file flat surfaces;
◆ round file to file round holes or curved surfaces;

◆ half-round file, which combines the features of the flat and round files;
◆ hand file, which has a safe and a live (toothed) edge;
◆ pillar file for filing narrow openings, a slimmer version of the hand file, with one safe edge;
◆ square file for use on rectangular slots. Some have three toothed sides and one safe side;
◆ mill file for fine work and sharpening the blades of circular saws; an all-purpose finishing file;
◆ triangular file for filing sharp recesses with acute internal angles. It clean cuts square corners;
◆ knife file for filing very acute angles with its knife-like edge;
◆ wood file for finishing wood with coarse file teeth (could be considered a rasp);
◆ needle files – miniatures of full-sized files and invaluable for tidying up corners and slots in work;
◆ surform round file – a hollow rasp perforated with sharp-edged holes along the blade's length, used to cut away wood rapidly;
◆ surform flat file, with perforated sharp-edged holes along the blade's length, used to cut away wood rapidly.

The **surform plane** works on the same principle as the surform file and is indispensable for the rough shaping of wood quickly. It is sold in two sizes: long with a handle and short, without.

The **cabinet rasp** removes wood quickly and is a coarser version of the half-round file with one flat and one rounded edge. The **flat wood rasp** is a coarse version of the round file, and shapes tightly curved wood.

Power rotary files and **rasps** are mounted on shanks for power drills. They can be bought separately or in sets. They do most of the work of hand files and rasps, but much more quickly. The coarse rasps should only be used on wood, not metal. They are cylindrical, cone and ball-shaped.

Miniature grindstones are mounted on steel shafts, which fit into the chuck of a drill. They come in three shapes: point, wheel and ball.

Engineer's pliers are used for gripping and bending sheet metal and cutting wire. The cropping sections are near the pivot, while the side cutters are positioned behind the serrated jaws. **Snipe-nosed pliers** are for gripping small objects in confined spaces. **Round-nosed pliers** are for bending wire into loops. **End cutting pliers** with rounded jaws are for cutting wire close to the surface and extracting nails.

Diagonal wire cutters are for cutting wire close to the surface. The most powerful force is generated just in front of the pivot. **Straight snips** are for cutting metal and lead sheets. They have long handles and long jaws in line with them, to enable cutting on a straight line.

Mole grips, with or without serrated jaws, are for strongly gripping sheet metal and tubular metal. When the handles are closed, great force is applied in a locked position. Only when the reverse lever is released is the pressure relaxed. It is, in fact, a miniature vice. There are various models, fulfilling many different functions, on the market, so be careful to select what you need. A broad and a narrow pair should suffice.

A **miniature modelling drill** provides most of the accessories found in a full-sized power tool kit: drill bits, grindstones, cutting wheels, drum sanders and wire brushes. They can be inserted into collets that fit the chuck. In use, the drill can be held in the hand or mounted on a miniature drill stand. A model of variable speed is recommended.

The well-known brand name **X-Acto** clearly describes the qualities of its **carving set**. All sorts of small gouges, knives, saws and chisels can be collected as blades, to fit into a tool handle with a securing knurled chuck. Full-sized chisels and gouges are beyond the scope of this book, since they are mainly for woodcarving and turning, but the X-Acto set fits the remit exactly.

The **modeller's knife** has a 'pencil' handle with a knurled chuck, like the X-Acto tool, and takes a series of gouges and miniature saws and blades. A **surgeon's scalpel** with a variety of blades in packets is useful for light-duty, very precise cutting. A **trimming knife** (Stanley knife) has disposable razor-sharp blades, which can be stored in the housing. A retractable blade is a safety advantage. A **putty knife** is for shaping and smoothing putty, but its use for the woodworker is its capacity to prise apart glued pieces of wood. A **filling knife** is used for spreading fillers in wood or plaster. This slightly flexible spatula has also the capacity to prise apart glued panels. A **palette knife** (small) is useful for mixing glue and sawdust to make your own filler, or for mixing two-part adhesives.

A **nail set** (punch) is for tapping nails and pins beneath the surface for filling, if you want them to be invisible. A **revolving head punch** punches out six different-sized holes in leather or any soft material. A revolving punch wheel lines up the hole you require with a metal stud on the lower jaw.

Awls and **bradawls** are used for making starter holes for screws and nails in wood. Always twist, and don't pierce too hard or the wood will split.

A **spanner** has closer connections to plumbing than making automata and, unless you are building your pieces with nuts and bolts, you will hardly use one. However, an adjustable spanner is a prerequisite for any tool kit.

Miscellaneous items that you may need include spray adhesive, compasses, dividers, protractors, set squares, glass cutters, spirit level and a Swiss Army penknife.

MATERIALS

Choosing materials is very different from choosing tools. While tools give endless service (unless they are power tools, which have a limited working life), materials are ephemeral, and need constant replenishing. Fundamentally, all makers use the same materials, but a host of different tools. The relationship between tools and the maker is based on trust and experience. They can be relied on, for the most part, to perform the functions for which they are intended. However, materials can be capricious, especially wood, which can split, crack or swell, shrink, warp or twist. For this reason, you should examine materials carefully before you purchase, and store them in dry conditions. Be very 'picky'. Wood yards will cut timber to size for you and they are cheaper than DIY shops.

Woods and Other Materials

Softwood is timber from coniferous trees with needle-like leaves. **Deal**, sold for shelving, is popular and easy to work. Splits in wood and unsightly knotting are common characteristics of the wood, but should be avoided. Planed timber sizes are machined smooth for final finishing by you.

Hardwood, being more resistant to surface scratching and bruising, is used for furniture making and is more expensive than softwood. You need sharp tools to work it. **Lime** and **beech** are ideal for carving.

Plywood is made, mostly, from an odd number of constructional veneers, bonded face to face with the grain running in alternate directions. This helps to prevent warping by equalizing the tensions on the odd-numbered veneers, which range from 3 ply to 19 multi-ply. **Birch ply** is recommended. Very thin ply called Aero (skin) ply is also available. Check the edges of ply board for gaps that have been filled but, nevertheless, run right through the board.

MDF (medium-density fibre) is popular because it is smooth on both sides and free from the defects that are found in ply. There is no splitting of the edge fibres when the board is cut and it never has any nasty surprises. MDF could be accused of being bland, with no interesting grain, but it can be painted and finished like ply. A mask should be worn when cutting MDF.

Battens (PSE) are bought in 6ft and 8ft (1.8 and 2.4m) lengths of softwood. You should keep a stock of various sizes to cover future projects. They measure from 2in to 4in (51mm to 102mm) thick and 5in to 8in (127mm to 203mm) wide.

Scantling is 2in to 4in (51mm to 102mm) thick and 2in to 5in (51mm to 127mm) wide. Thinner stripwood can be purchased in model shops and DIY stores.

Dowel rods, available from model shops and DIY shops, are usually made from hardwood. They start from very small diameters and go up to 1in (25mm). Broom handles are ideal for cutting cams, preferably without the broom head attached!

Abrasives

Abrasives come in three grades: coarse, medium and fine, with finer subdivisions within each grade, denoted by numbers. **Flint** or **glasspaper** is the cheapest abrasive. It wears out quickly and is used for finishing rough timber. Being yellow, it is often confused with sandpaper, which is no longer made. **Emery paper**, with either a paper or cloth backing, is mainly for finishing metal. It can be used dry. **Garnet paper**, also used dry, is coloured red and backed with paper, and is used for hand-finishing timber. **Synthetic silicon carbide** (wet and dry) is harder than emery, with a waterproof paper backing that allows it to be used wet to finish paint or metal. Paper- and cloth-backed **aluminium oxide** is used for machine-sanding wood or metal. **Tungsten carbide** is the hardest abrasive, mainly used in sanding machines. It is sold in strips and the cast-off (used) lighter grades are very useful, because they are so hard-wearing.

A **sanding block** is used for finishing flat surfaces. It does by hand what a power belt sander or orbital sander does mechanically. Buy them ready-made or make your own by sticking a piece of cork to a block and wrapping an abrasive around it.

Adhesives

Adhesives are a matter of personal preference, but the following three different glues for different occasions should cover all eventualities:

- **PVA** (polyvinylacetate) is for general purposes. It is white in colour but dries clear. Evo-Stick Wood Adhesive (Weatherproof) is one example.
- **Epoxy resin** is a two-part waterproof adhesive (with hardener), which bonds wood, metal or glass very strongly, with no shrinkage. Araldite (Rapid) is one example.
- **Cellulose** (cyanoacrylate) is an instant glue that is sold in thick and thin solutions. It is effective for instant bonding when thin, and workable for a very short time when thick. Zap and Grip both bond wood, metal and glass. It is very dangerous for children, who should not be allowed near it.

Miscellaneous

Fillers are used for correcting errors in work. What used to be known as 'plastic wood' is sold as various stoppers, but it is relatively easy to make your own. Mix up sawdust and PVA glue with a palette knife, and apply it so that it is proud of the hole to be filled, because it will shrink. It will dry dark, so will need to be painted over.

Plastic padding (for example, Loctite Chemical Metal) is a two-part (with hardener) compound, grey in colour, which bonds and fills wood, metal and glass. It dries rock hard in ten minutes and can then be drilled, sanded and painted. It is especially useful if you have to fill and redrill a hole that was slightly out of position.

Milliput is a two-part versatile putty (with hardener), which adheres to and will seal ceramics, wood, plastics, glass and metal. It is sold in model and art shops in white (for mending ceramics) and grey, which is cheaper. Once set it can be sawn, drilled, filed, sanded, painted or cellulose-sprayed. Store unused mixed Milliput in the fridge.

Screws are more efficient for gripping timber than nails, which rely entirely on friction for bonding power. The main advantage to the automatist is that work that is screwed is not sealed for ever. Remember always to leave an 'escape hatch', which can be removed if it is screwed in. When ordering screws you need to know the head style (flat, countersunk or Pozidrive), the gauge, length, material and type of finish.

Panel pins are for fixing ply or mouldings. They can be punched below the surface and range from ½in to 2in (13mm to 50mm). **Veneer pins** are smaller versions of panel pins ranging from ⅜in to 1½in (10mm to 38mm). **Gimp pins** are small brass panel pins which are rust-resistant, ranging from ⅜in to ¾in (10mm to 19mm).

Hinges are available in brass, steel and nylon and generally supplied in pairs. Most small and miniature hinges are made from solid-drawn brass. They need countersunk screws, which should be sold with them.

MAKERS' WORK

John Maltby

*I've made automata for many years, hopefully
with an attitude of relaxation from my main
concern as a ceramic maker. Though there have
been frightening exceptions (perhaps revealing
my subconscious thoughts to myself more clearly
than I might wish!) the overall spirit of such
mechanisms seems to have veered towards the
wryly amusing and gently frivolous – aspects
which coincide perfectly with my soporific aim!
Just as there is no viciousness in Tipoo's tiger
savaging his human prey (a frightening and
influential object in my younger days), my
boats are not threatened by the storms through
which they battle manfully – they return rhyth-
mically to the safe haven of the harbour.*

*The innocence of such objects (and their
simple mechanisms) is important: though various rather more serious influences can be rec-
ognized – the works of Nicholson, Paul Klee
and Alfred Wallis, for instance – their real
purpose is innocent pleasure. Hopefully – in
an age obsessed with technological invention –
they are non-taxing in their abject simplicity.*

'Rocking Fish Clock' was made in varied
editions about 1990. It has a simple pendulum motion and measures 203 ×
305mm (8 × 12in).

'Four Boats Returning to Harbour' was
made in painted wood in 1992. A simple
push-pull mechanism rocks the sailing
boats. It measures 610 × 305mm (24 ×
12in).

'Peter Grimes Sailing off Aldeburgh' is an
imaginary seascape in painted wood, mixing various English allusions. It uses a
pendulum motion and measures 457 ×
457mm (18 × 18in). 1998.

'Three Yachts Racing' uses another simple
push-pull mechanism to rock the yachts.
It measures 24 × 14in (610 × 356mm).
1998.

In 'The Proposal' the man's arm offers (and
retracts!) the bouquet to his intended in a
pulling mechanism. The piece measures
254 × 305mm (10 × 12in). 1999.

*'Four Boats Returning
to Harbour', 1992
(610 × 305mm/
24 × 12in).*

*'Rocking Fish Clock' by
John Maltby, 1990
(203 × 305mm/8 × 12in).*

ABOVE LEFT: 'Peter Grimes Sailing off Aldeburgh', 1998 (457 × 457mm/18 × 18in).

ABOVE: 'The Proposal', 1999 (254 × 305mm/ 10 × 12in).

LEFT: 'Three Yachts Racing', 1998 (610 × 356mm/24 × 14in).

'SS Caruso' by Tony Mann, 2001 (500 × 600mm/20 × 24in).

Tony Mann

Tony Mann specializes in making automata and moving toys for adult collectors, working mainly in painted wood. He has produced several hundred different designs since he began to make craft toys and automata in 1975. He has exhibited widely in art galleries and craft centres throughout the UK.

While much of his production has been one-of-a-kind or short-run pieces for sale to collectors, he has also received major commissions to make automata for institutional and commercial clients, which have usually taken several months to make.

I started making toys in 1974 after working for over twenty years as a designer. Now I am perhaps better known for making automata. These are usually operated by winding handles and give me an opportunity to indulge what people have called my quirky sense of humour. I prefer making new pieces and exploring fresh ideas although I still do short runs of smaller toys. My larger pieces can take three to four months to make and have generally been commissioned by galleries and museums for children's exhibitions.

Although my work is mostly shown in art and craft galleries I prefer to be thought of as a toymaker, because fine art takes itself so seriously. Folk art is what I really enjoy and many of my pieces use the bright colours and rough finish that I admire in toys from South America, India and Japan. I love to retain some of that quality in my own work.

The vernacular and industrial crafts have always appealed to me more than polite art and I enjoy visiting museums more than art galleries for that reason. The machines, tools, toys and advertising of the nineteenth century, for example, often have that sense of having been made by individuals who cared about their work and wanted to put something of themselves into their products, no matter how mundane or humble their use. That is why I enjoy hunting through second-hand shops and junk yards for things that I might be able to incorporate into my pieces.

During the past two years, for instance, I have been making a series of wooden fishes, which use corroded metal, blistered paint and recycled junk, to explore relationships between the useful and the useless. Some are montaged with old documents or technical drawings; some have machine parts or rusted hardware; some look as though they have been found on the seashore. Most have numbers or lettering of some sort. They hint at functions which are unclear, enigmatic and ambiguous.

By keeping to the same theme, I was free to concentrate on making each fish as different as possible by experimenting with new techniques. Some use decorative painted finishes, which contrasted organic and geometric forms; others use cast-metal textures. They don't do much except wag their tails, open their mouths and look silly in a serious sort of way. They are equally happy hanging on walls or standing on shelves. And they don't need feeding.

ABOVE: 'Circus', 1993 (700 × 120cm/23ft × 3ft 11in).

'Blue Enamel Fish', 2000 (600 × 460mm/24 × 18in).

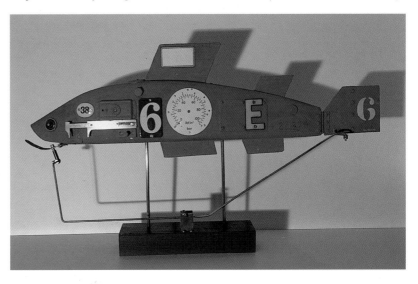

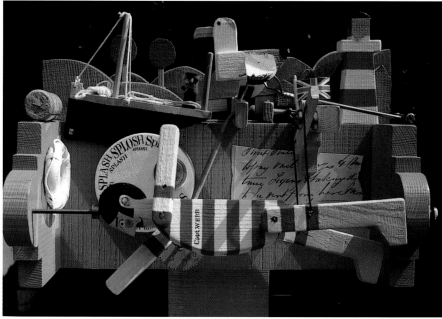

LEFT: 'Moo Machine' by Tony Mann, 1990 (410 × 600mm/16 × 24in).

'Splish, Splash, Splosh' by Tony Mann, 1993 (300 × 340mm/12 × 13½in).

Peter Markey

I have always been making things, for as long as I can remember. If you make something, you exist and feel good. I love solving problems and reducing everything to only necessary details. The great excitement is starting with a blank page and not knowing what you will come up with, except that it will be a regurgitation of what you have done before. I try not to be aware of how others solve problems. I just like finding my own way and making my own rules. I think that this is the result of teaching art and crafts for twenty-five years, using methods which enabled every child to be successful. When I have finished something I say to myself, 'Now what improvements can I make, what can I leave out?' I go to sleep at night trying to come up with an idea, and wake up enthusiastically still having to do it. It is also exceedingly pleasant completing something reasonably successfully.

Peter Markey was born in Swansea in 1930. After studying at the local art college he moved to London to begin a teaching career. Later he moved to Falmouth, Cornwall, and, after twenty-five years of teaching, began to concentrate on his own work.

Markey's work is always simple and decorative. He uses the most basic mechanical means to move his models, making the working mechanics visually important. He first makes rough sketches and then an approximate-scale working drawing, culminating, generally, in a full-scale drawing. In the process of making a model, new ideas come to light. These can lead to small changes and additions that are improvements on the original design.

All Markey's machines are usually made entirely out of wood, mostly softwoods such as deal, because they are light, and lightness is strength. Axles are made from hardwood dowels with resin bearings.

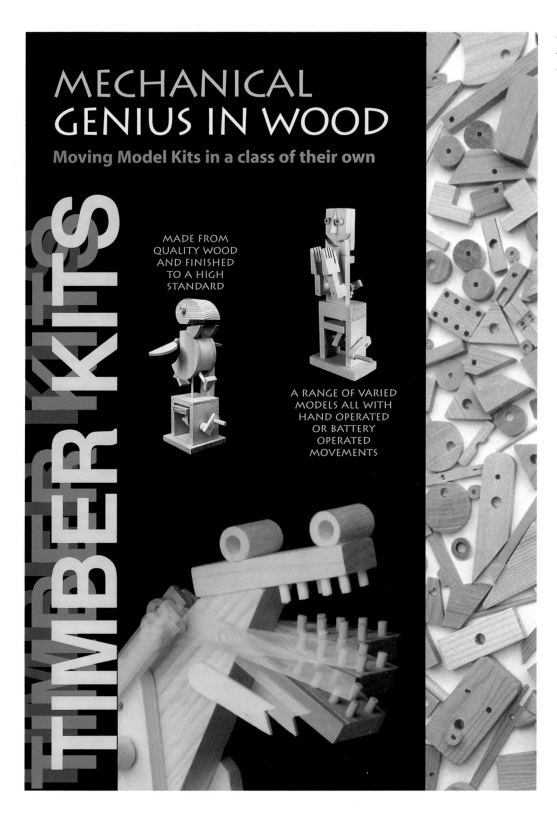

Front cover of Peter Markey's 'Timber Kits' folder.

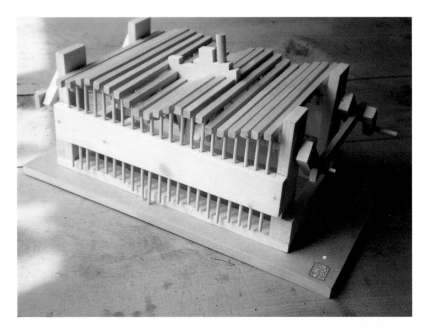

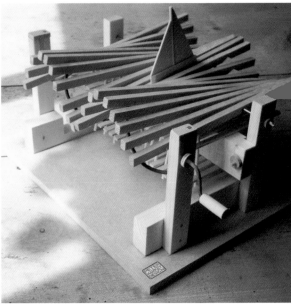

'Wave Machines' by Peter Markey, 1990–96.

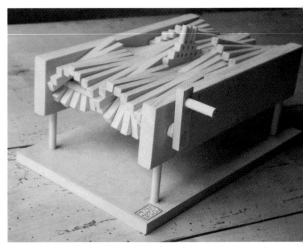

4 TECHNIQUES

TECHNIQUES AND TECHNIQUE

'Techniques' are technical working methods, or tricks of the trade, which, if they don't actually improve your work, will none the less make it easier to do. 'Technique' in the singular is the manual dexterity acquired with experience, which will improve your work. Beginners should save a lot of time and trouble by taking note of the tips given here, acquiring in just a few minutes the kind of knowledge that would have taken years to gather by experience.

All makers have their own methods of working, just as they have their own favourite tools and materials; but one thing they all have in common is technique. Each maker's own technique shapes not only the pieces they make but the particular ways in which they make them. It is something that grows with the maker, like a collection of tools. Makers learn to apply techniques they have acquired whether from others or by empirical means, just as they select a particular tool for a particular part of a particular job. Technique, like design and aesthetics, is all part of their own particular artistry.

Sometimes, technique can get in the way of creativity, creeping forward to play the leading role, when it should be no more than a featured player. Too much emphasis on technique obliterates the main purpose of the piece being made. The message becomes the messenger and consequently it doesn't get through.

A piece should be the result of using head, heart and hand – in that order. The head receives ideas, the heart engenders passion to realize those ideas and the hand fashions them into the work. As long as the pecking order is maintained, then the message will get through. If the order is mixed up or reversed, it will show in the work. Ideally, there should be a distribution of creative input for all three categories, the ratios to be decided by the individual. Too much head will generate labyrinthine ideas; too much heart will produce sugary sentimentality; and too much hand will supply a glut of technique.

'HOW TO'

Transferring Designs

Transferring designs on to wood can be done in three different ways, depending on the nature of the design:

1. Trace the design on to tracing paper with an HB pencil. Turn over the tracing paper so that the drawing is facing the wood. Secure it with tape just at the top, so that you can lift the paper now and then to check that the design is transferring adequately. This is done with a burnisher or the back of a spoon handle. It won't matter that the image is reversed on the wood if you are only cutting shapes. However, if you need to show your design the right way round, with drawn details, for instance, then you should rub it on another piece of tracing paper and transfer that to be burnished on to the wood.

2. Following the above method, transfer the design on to thin card or plasticard, cut out the shapes and use them as templates for repeat work.

3. The simplest and quickest way is to take a fax or photocopy of the design. Spray the back very lightly with adhesive and

rub it gently on to the wood with the flat of the hand. If accuracy is important, ensure that there is no distortion of the print before applying it to the surface.

Using Powered Saws

Fretsaws or **scroll saws** must be used with the blade teeth pointing downwards. Press forward firmly but gently on the wood as you feed it past the blade. Let it find its own pace, and never force it through, as this may cause the blade to become blocked in the wood. This would invite scorch marks and possibly break the blade.

The teeth of woodcutting saws are set wider apart than those on saws used for metal cutting. Since the wood has a grain, closely set teeth might lock the fibres. The choice of blade should be governed by the work.

Cutting straight lines is easier if you score a line for the blade to follow. Just a slight cut in the wood favours the blade by making a path for it. A drawn line is simply not as efficient. Any irregularities can be sanded off at right-angles with the sanding block.

Cutting corners can be done in one continuous movement with very fine blades, but scorch marks might appear if the turn is too tight for the blade. To get the cleanest cuts in the corners it is best to approach them from two directions: leave your cutting line and make a 'loop detour' in the wood to make a new approach to the corner. If you are cutting out a rectangle, say, in a continuous line without making a 'loop detour', draw the blade back by the blade's thickness and turn the wood gently at right-angles till it faces in its new direction. This prevents locking and undue strain on the blade.

Cutting circles can be done with a hole saw, leaving a central hole, which can be filled if necessary. For larger circles, if you find difficulty in cutting absolutely accurately on a compass line, spin a second circle, a millimetre wider, and cut on that

line. Sand away the residue up to the inner circle compass line and a perfect circle should result.

Cutting interiors is done by drilling a hole large enough to receive a blade through it easily, to access an interior opening. Free the top of the blade and guide it through the drilled hole from under the wood. Tighten up the blade, ensuring that it is taut. A wavy blade gives a wavy cut. Once the opening has been cut away, release the blade and remove the work. Then tighten it up to resume normal cutting.

Plural cutting is a useful time-saver when two or more fairly thin pieces can be cut as one. Dab glue on to them to hold them together temporarily. This can be used to bind the pieces together but its success depends on the nature of the work.

Always cut in a good light, preferably facing a window. Ensure that the shadow of the blade does not fall on the cutting line. It is hard enough to follow one line perfectly, let alone two!

Drilling

The drill and drill stand must be compatible – most manufacturers' accessories fit only their own brand. Pillar drills, with an integral motor, are the most accurate. If your drill stand is not fitted with a depth-stop gauge, you can make your own by winding tape around the drill bit to act as a guide.

Drilling holes through wood is made easier if you place a piece of scrap wood under the piece you are drilling, to prevent splintering. (The main cause of splintering is a blunt drill bit.) Accurate drilling with a drill stand is best done with a succession of pressures rather than one downward thrust. This gives the drill bit more opportunity to run a straight course. The less the drill bit projects from the chuck, the more precise the drilling will be.

Pilot and **clearance holes** must be drilled for screws to grip and pass through the wood, locked by their heads. The ideal clearance hole for a No.8 screw, in softwood for example, is 2.5mm (³⁄₃₂in) and the pilot hole should be 1.5mm (¹⁄₁₆in). With hardwood, the diameters are increased to 4mm (⁵⁄₃₂in) and 2.5mm respectively.

Countersinking screws is necessary when you wish to hide the screwhead just below the surface. Either use a countersink bit or drill a hole to a shallow depth to accommodate the head. The hole is then slightly overfilled with a stopper, or a mixture of sawdust and glue, which keys into the slotted or Pozidrive screw head. Sand off flush when dry.

Holes can be **shrunk** by soaking them in hot water. Loose bearings and cams can be treated in this way. They will need sanding. To **widen holes**, gently apply pressure against the revolving drill bit, towards the four compass points, in rotation. Alternatively, a round needle file can be used.

Drilling holes in confined areas can split the wood. If you wish to drill a 4mm (⁵⁄₃₂in) hole in wood 6mm (¼in) wide, say, drill a 2mm (³⁄₃₂in) hole first followed by a 4mm hole to widen it. The wood will offer less resistance and will not split.

Drilling collets and **washers** is best done, a few at a time, through 25mm (1in) of dowel held in a clamp and then cut in sections. For a pillar drill this is no problem, but if you are using a drill stand, the hole may end up slightly off centre at the base. Only experimentation and practice can help here, unless you invest in a pillar drill. (For details of collets to cut, *see* Chapter 5 on mechanisms.) The alternative is to cut each collet and washer separately, which is quite difficult if they are small, as they need to be gripped while drilling. Sharp drill bits are essential for this if splitting is to be avoided. Ensure that your drill stand is firmly tightened up to improve performance.

Filling holes with dowel is an effective way of plugging them. Chamfer the end of the dowel to facilitate entry into the hole to be plugged. Tap it down with a light hammer so that it is flush with the surface, and

sand off. There is no need to glue, for this is the ultimate friction fit.

Power Sawing

Circular saws can come as attachments to power tools or integral models incorporating their own power units. The latter perform better and also avoid delays in fitting. Both types can be used freehand or in conjunction with a saw blade.

Always check for hidden nails and screws in the wood before sawing. Start the motor before you cut, or the saw will kick against the work, spoiling the edge. Ease the saw forward gently and never strain the motor. If it slows down, reduce the forward pressure and allow the saw to pick up speed again. If the blade jams in the wood it probably needs sharpening, which is best done by an expert.

The following types of circular saw blade are available:

- combination, for cutting with or across the grain;
- cross-cut, with smooth teeth, for cutting across the grain;
- rip, for coarse cutting with the grain; and
- planer, for clearing waste.

The thickness of these blades provides accuracy in cutting straight lines in timber from 25mm (1in) to 75mm (3in). Once you have fitted a blade, ensure that the adjustable sole plate is set for 90-degree cutting.

Jigsaws are not as fast and accurate as circular saws but they are much more versatile and compact. They offer a number of blades, for cutting wood, metal and plastics, and they can cut curves with blades that are specially designed for the purpose. Always check that the adjustable sole plate is set at 90 degrees. Since the jigsaw cuts on the upstroke it leaves a smoother cut on the underside of the work. Take care not to saw into the work bench or support.

Sanding

Sanding is the tedious part of woodwork, but it can be speeded up by the use of power sanders. There are four types of sander:

1. The orbital sander is for fine sanding and not to be used for removing quantities of material.
2. The belt sander is expensive but very effective for removing material and giving a fine finish.
3. The disc sander is a drill attachment in the form of a flexible rubber disc. It should be held at 30 degrees to work efficiently. Never try to use it flat or you will make deep circular grooves, which are tedious to remove.
4. The drum sander is a small drill attachment for sanding curved and straight surfaces.

Sand along the grain where possible. Work through the grades of abrasives: coarse, medium and fine. Final sanding can be done by hand.

Miscellaneous Techniques and Tips

The **removal of bruises** is generally successful on softwood, but a little more difficult on hardwood. You need boiling water, cotton wool and plenty of cloth. Make a firm pad of cotton wool and wrap it in a cloth, securing it by a knot that you can hold. Soak the pad in boiling water and apply to the bruise. Wipe off all excess water. Keep the water boiling throughout repeated applications until the bruise has gone. Leave it to dry out and then sand it with a fine abrasive.

Cutting dowel with a mitre saw can sometimes result in rough fibres being left. To rectify this, twist the dowel every few strokes so that the whole circumference has been cut before the dowel is finally severed.

Measuring is the basis for all projects. There is one golden rule: measure a thousand times, cut only once. The ruler is your closest friend. It tells you the truth, not approximately, but exactly.

Unsticking glued pieces can result in breaking fibres, if PVA adhesive is used. If you think you may need to reposition small pieces, use an instant glue, which, though strong, will not key into the wood so firmly. Protecting it with a bit of scrap wood, knock off the piece briskly with a light hammer. The fibres should remain intact.

Cutting piano wire with clippers can result in the cut piece shooting off like a bullet. If it is tiny, it may become irretrievably lost, so put a bag over it to restrain it. Wear gardening gloves if you find cutting difficult.

Making **pin wheels** with pins of all the same height is done by wrapping masking tape around them to the required length. Using a power sander, sand off the metal up to the tape.

Candle grease will facilitate action in moving wooden parts. It will also quieten unwanted squeaks.

Lead weights for counterbalancing moving parts can be cut from roofing lead found on building sites; ask a friendly builder for scraps and use snips to cut them.

Friction fit is the means by which the building and dismantling of mechanisms featured here is made possible. Much of the work is held together by pegs, which can be fitted or pulled apart for assembly or reassembly. It is an ideal method for making prototypes when you want to keep the work in a fluid, unfixed state.

Working on **acetate or cel** is ideal for glueing small parts in position over a cutting mat with a grid. Its transparency allows both visibility of the grid and protection of the surface from glue without sticking to the work as paper would. This method is recommended for making camshafts, using the grid as a guide to keep the work square.

A **drill bits gauge** can be made by drilling holes in a piece of plywood, in sequence with their measurements marked. Make one for imperial and one for metric, or combine the two on one piece of ply.

MAKERS' WORK

Ian McKay

I trained as a ceramicist, although I've always enjoyed using different materials. I've been a silversmith, a blacksmith, furniture designer, a maker of wood engraving blocks, drummer, technician, teacher, gardener, and full-time suburban being. Toymaking seems to be the sum of all these experiences. One of the most important days of my life was spent at the Sam Smith/H.C. Westerman exhibition at the Serpentine Gallery in the early 1980s. To quote my three-year-old son, 'It knocked me down with a feather'. But it took ten years to realize that I could become a toymaker. My first efforts were tiny moving boats made from wire and old matchboxes. A stint working in a highly automated chicken factory whetted my appetite for things mechanical.

My recent work has been done amidst mayhem – since parenthood came my way I have worked in the extended litter of an ebullient toddler. What was once subtitled Art House is now Disney. Trips to the Serpentine are now trips to Bristol Zoo. Radio 1 is now Radio 2 although the presenters are still the same. And as noisy electronic toys go off sporadically around me, I – still working in the twentieth or even the nineteenth century – use wood, brass rod and paint. The effect of all this is that I have become much more interested in people and their emotions and the absurdities of living.

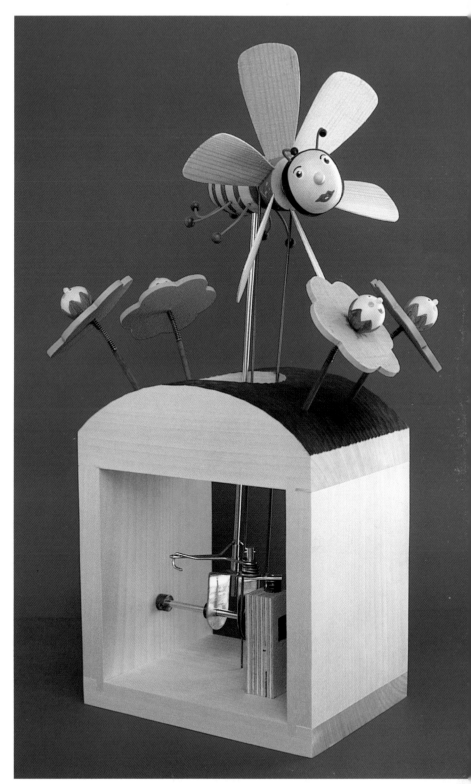

'W.A.S.P.', 1999 (450mm/18in).

'Pink Lady and Blue Poodles' by Ian McKay, 2000 (350mm/14in).

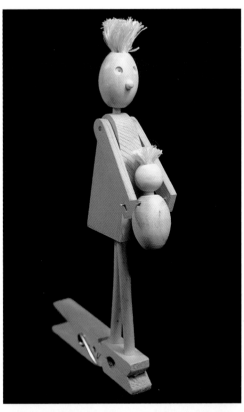

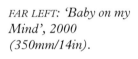

FAR LEFT: 'Baby on my Mind', 2000 (350mm/14in).

LEFT: 'Peg Baby', 2000 (120mm/4¾in).

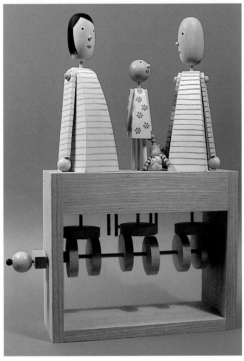

'Gossip', 2000 (250mm/9¾in).

Frank Nelson

Automata give the artist the extra dimension of time to tell its story or perform its intended function.

A respect for the work of the sixteenth-century Nuremburg woodcarvers, combined with a fascination with the amazing possibilities of simple logical mechanisms, drives my work. I use a different mechanical principle in each piece. My childhood was spent in Blackpool in the 1930s. Many amusement machines then were animated scenes: 'The Drunkard's Dream' and 'The Haunted House', and so on. At art school I became hooked on motorbikes, so spent the next ten years in various forms of engineering, eventually starting my own industrial model-making business. At one time I was making weapons for the film Star Wars *and all the cockpit instruments for what is now the 'Tornado' fighter-bomber – I then had a breakdown.*

The only way out of this for me was to carve and animate wooden figures. After I had made a number of these, a film about Sam Smith appeared on television. I wrote to Sam and we arranged to meet in 1977. He was the nicest man I have ever known. After seeing some of my things he said, 'This is the way I wanted to work, but I don't have the mechanical ability.' Imagine how I felt hearing that from the man whose work I had enjoyed since the 1940s! Sam told me to submit for the Summer Show at the Serpentine Gallery in Hyde Park. He must have had a word, for when I went there to show my work, the curator said, 'Can I buy that one? And which gallery would you like?' The show was a great success and led to many exhibitions and opportunities as a visiting tutor at a number of colleges, including Parnham House, where I enjoyed many years working with students of such high standard.

Now in my seventies, I spend most of my time drawing and painting, but I am still working on a limited edition acrobatic automaton.

'The Tamer' (1978) is made in carved and painted wood and is hand-operated. Performance time is approximately 45 seconds and its size is 510 × 280 × 180mm (20 × 11 × 7in).

I see this as my trademark piece. The tamer cracks his whip and gets a refusal each time from the tiger, who shakes his head from side to side while his tail rotates. On the third crack of the whip, however, the tiger accepts the command, nods his head and does his trick – putting his head into the trainer's mouth.

'Queen Victoria' (1988) is made in carved and painted wood and is hand-operated. Performance time is 15 seconds and its size is 710 × 350 × 350mm (28 × 14 × 14in). The action starts with a loud fart and a reaction from the Queen's eyes and the ears of the Skye Terrier. She tells her servant, 'Stop that, James', to which he replies, 'Yes ma'am, which way did it go?' 'Queen Victoria' works on the principle of a lever operating one mechanism one way and a different mechanism on its return.

'The Cow' (1994) is made in carved and painted wood. It is wall-mounted and hand-operated, and measures 500 × 470 × 390mm (20 × 18½ × 15in). When the cow's horn is cranked, the cow moos and dispenses one Oxo cube before winking on the return stroke. It works using a simple lever action.

'The Flasher Judge' (1976), in carved and painted wood, is hand-operated. There is a great facial change from a single action.

'The American Eagle' (1972), in carved and painted wood, is wall-mounted and hand-operated. Its size is 370 × 820 × 140mm (14½ × 32 × 5½in). This piece was carved as an exercise and then animated after a visit to America. A pull cord raises the figure, who sits astride the eagle waving her burning bra! The pull cord spins a flywheel, which gives action to the woman's arm.

'The Tamer' by Frank Nelson, 1978 (510 × 280 × 180mm/20 × 11 × 7in).

RIGHT: 'Queen Victoria', 1988 (710 × 350 × 350mm/28 × 14 × 14in).

FAR RIGHT: 'The Cow', 1994 (500 × 470 × 390mm/20 × 18½ × 15in).

RIGHT: 'The Flasher Judge', 1976.

FAR RIGHT: 'The American Eagle', 1972 (370 × 820 × 140mm/14½ × 32 × 5½in).

Keith Newstead

I like my pieces to have a smooth movement with the occasional sudden crash. I don't take myself too seriously. I like automata because they don't really fit into the established roles of arts and crafts. That's the attraction.

Keith Newstead studied art and design, with a view to a career in graphic design. He soon decided, however, that this was not for him and spent some time travelling and doing casual jobs before beginning to make a living in the craft world. He was inspired by a television documentary about the late Sam Smith to start a career as an automata maker.

Newstead's work is mostly made from burnished metal sheet and wire, with various cogs and mechanisms proudly displayed as an integral part of each piece. His colourful creations reveal a fanciful, humorous imagination, as well as a meticulous dedication to detail and a great talent for engineering in miniature.

Keith Newstead lives and works in Falmouth, Cornwall.

Keith Newstead working on his 'Submarine (Under the Sea)', 1992 (508 × 508 × 330mm/20 × 20 × 13in).

'Junkas Giles Agriplane' by Keith Newstead, 1993 (483 × 254 × 254mm/ 19 × 10 × 10in).

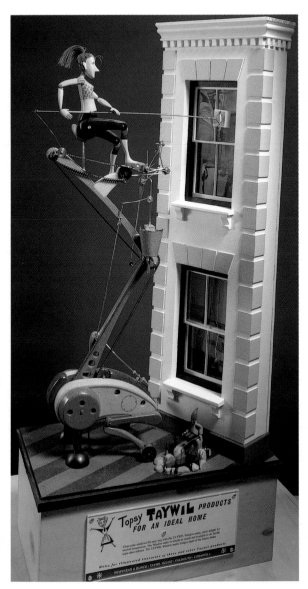

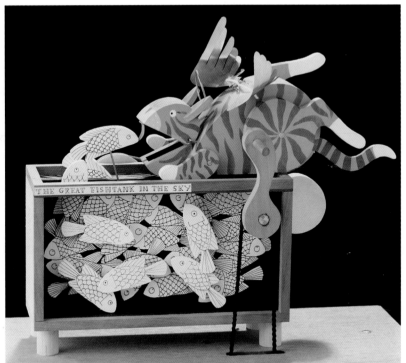

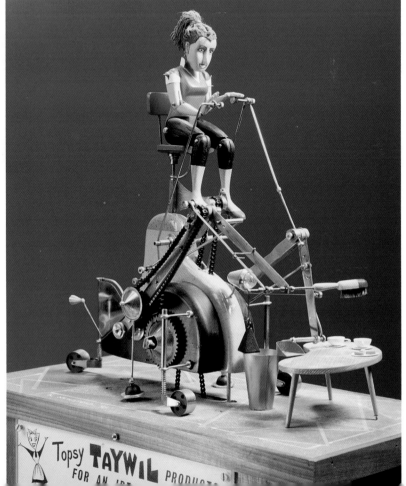

ABOVE: 'Window Cleaner', 1998 (483 × 280 × 127mm/19 × 11 × 5in).

ABOVE RIGHT: 'Great Fish Tank in the Sky', 1994 (203 × 127 × 64mm/8 × 5 × 2½in).

'Dust-O-Matic', 1997 (356 × 152 × 356mm/14 × 6 × 14in).

The bearings box, with a full cast of cams, followers, weights and a friction-driven flagpole.

5 MAKING AUTOMATA MECHANISMS

The photographs and diagrams here should provide enough information to give a working knowledge of mechanisms, but the best way to understand what a mechanism can do for you is to make it or see it working. Only then can you really appreciate the action and relate it to the movement you wish to create. Indeed, the mechanism itself may suggest an idea for a piece. There is no substitute for actually handling and operating automata. One way of doing this is through buying one of the cheap wooden kits, or even paper ones, that are on the market. Peter Markey has designed a number of these, wonderfully simple examples of the

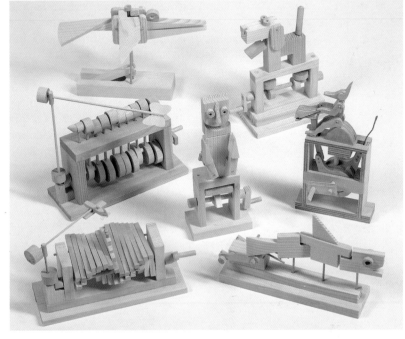

automatist's art. Paul Spooner has designed the ingenious Camel Simulator (*see* photo above and drawing left).

To learn more about automata and mechanical toys, follow the step-by-step instructions of how to make the mechanisms and discover what they do. All the main movements for making automata are described here. Their mechanisms are designed to be assembled and dismantled, by friction fit, on to the bearings box, which houses the shaft. Clearly, there are many tiny bits and pieces to make and assemble, and it is important not to muddle them up, so they have been coloured for identification. Also each piece, even down to the last washer, is numbered, to correspond to a section in the 'box of mechanisms' that houses them. For the plans for making the

ABOVE: There are a number of simple kits available that are ideal for learning about mechanisms. Most were designed by Peter Markey and made by Eric and Alison Williamson, who also designed and made 'The Caterpillar'. 'Anubis Riding Simulated Camel' is by Paul Spooner and marketed by Cabaret Mechanical Theatre.

FAR LEFT: Plan for the Camel Simulator kit, designed by Paul Spooner for CMT.

a *whiff of Old Egypt in a kit*

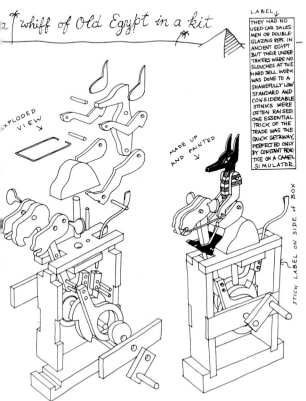

LABEL ↓

THEY HAD NO USED-CAR SALES-MEN OR DOUBLE-GLAZING REPS. IN ANCIENT EGYPT BUT THEIR UNDER-TAKERS WERE NO SLOUCHES AT THE HARD SELL. WORK WAS DONE TO A SHAMEFULLY LOW STANDARD AND CONSIDERABLE STINKS WERE OFTEN RAISED ONE ESSENTIAL TRICK OF THE TRADE WAS THE QUICK GETAWAY, PERFECTED ONLY BY CONSTANT PRAC-TICE ON A CAMEL SIMULATOR.

EXPLODED VIEW

MADE UP AND PAINTED ↓

STICK LABEL ON SIDE OF BOX

box, *see* page 109. As the sections are built to the interior height of the box, the pieces are kept safely within them.

For simplicity, **the plans show wood thicknesses in millimetres only**. For imperial/metric conversions, *see* the table on page 116.

The bearings box, crank handle and shaft, which appear on Plan 1, are basic mechanisms that are used throughout, but they are not reproduced on every plan. Similarly, the plinth, which appears on Plan 8 for four-bar-linkage, is too large to reproduce more than once. Therefore, when making the ratchet (Plan 10), pin wheels (Plan 13), and the friction-driven pole (Plan 14), you should refer to Plan 8 for making the plinth.

The bearings box and shaft and crank handle.

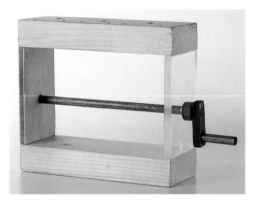

BEARINGS AND SHAFTS

The bearings box acts as a proscenium throughout for the mechanical activity provided by a cast of cams, cogs, levers, ratchets and wheels. As on a stage, where actors do not all come on at once, the mechanical participants will make their appearances separately or together, as the performance dictates.

A star in the troupe of mechanisms is surely the crank pin, with its eccentrically positioned pin on the wheel attached to the shaft. It plays a pivotal role in the four-bar linkage, the bell crank and all ratchets, including the Geneva wheel. The function of the bearings box is to support, at either end, a rotating shaft that plays a more ubiquitous, though less showy, role than the crank pin.

For light wooden automata and mechanical toys, you need to drill a hole slightly larger than the diameter of the shaft in the two sides of the bearings box, temporarily bonded together. This ensures accuracy when the dowel shaft rotates in the bearings.

Shafts can be made from piano wire or even coat hangers, which can be bent to make crank handles. Brass tubing can add strength to the bearings.

Rotation is not the only motion for a shaft, which can also move up and down in its bearing. For this reason, the top of the bearings box is much thicker than the sides. It allows the vertical bearing to contain the moving shaft, discouraging drift or jamming.

Making the Bearings Box
1. Cut two side panels A, from 5mm thick plywood, temporarily bonding them. Then drill a hole to fit a 5mm dowel shaft, so that it can move freely, not too loosely or snugly, within the bearing. Separate the sides and sand off.
2. Cut the top B and base C, from $^{13}/_{16} \times 1^{3}/_{4}$in (20 × 44mm) baton. Drill holes, as indicated on Plan 1, right through the top, B. Drill holes to a depth of 17mm in the underside of the base B. The large holes are bearings for pin and roller followers (*see* page 80, on cams and followers). The small holes will house pegs for fixtures with a friction fit.
3. Now glue the two sides A, to support the top B, and to rest on the base C. Ensure that all is square otherwise the shaft will not work smoothly in the bearings.
4. Cut the four pegs F for the base and the plinth (*see* Plan 8) for four-bar linkage.

Making the Shaft
1. Cut a long and a short dowel for the shaft D and crank handle. Drill two holes into the 5mm × 10mm stripwood for them.

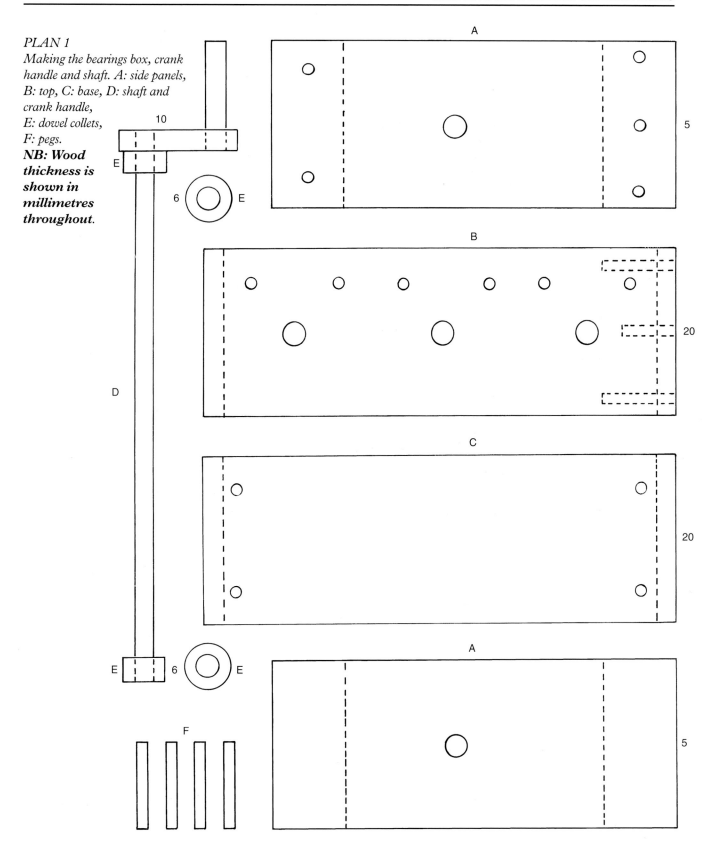

PLAN 1
Making the bearings box, crank handle and shaft. A: side panels, B: top, C: base, D: shaft and crank handle, E: dowel collets, F: pegs.
NB: Wood thickness is shown in millimetres throughout.

2. Cut two dowels E, 12mm in diameter and 6mm thick. Drill central holes into these to fit the shaft tightly. One should be glued, with the handle, to the shaft. The other serves as a friction-fit collet at the end.

3. Ensure that the shaft moves smoothly between the bearings. These can shrink in damp or cold weather, so allow enough, but not too much, play in the bearings.

The five green cams will all work with the green pin follower and the two plain disc followers. The perspex shield gives added stability to the pin follower and its block.

The five red cams will all work with the red roller follower and the two plain disc followers. The perspex shield takes the strain off the roller mechanism by steadying the block on top of the shaft.

CAMS AND FOLLOWERS

Cams are shaped pieces of wood, metal or plastic, which are fixed to a rotating shaft. They can be linear or rotary. The rotary type is much more usual, changing rotary motion into either reciprocating or oscillating motion. Some are called lobed cams because they have lobes added on to the disc shape.

The follower hugs the profile or radial surface of the cam. It does this either by gravity or by the aid of a spring. The more precise the follower, such as a roller or a pin follower, the more accurate the projection or movement will be. Therefore, although disc followers should never jam (never say 'never'!), they follow cam profiles only roughly.

The rotary cam shown on the cam templates plan (*see* opposite) is probably the most popular, since it can be cut from a dowel rod. It is called the circular eccentric cam, because the disc is fitted off-centre on the shaft. It lifts and drops the follower in one continuous movement.

The shape and size of cam dictates the amount of movement and distance covered by the follower. It also determines whether or not it can turn both clockwise and anti-clockwise. In Plan 2 (*see* opposite), which shows cam templates, A and B can only turn in one direction. It is most important, therefore, when designing a piece, to know the limitations of the cams you wish to use.

COLOUR AND
NUMBER THE PARTS

Cam Templates
The cams in the photos left give a good variation of movement. Each provides activities that can only be really appreciated by cutting the 8mm thick cams from plywood, temporarily bonding them to the shaft, and seeing how they work. Remember that these mechanisms are designed to be dismantled

PLAN 2
Making cam templates. A, B, C, D and E will work with a pin follower. F, G, H, I and J will only work efficiently with a roller follower. All cams work with disc followers.

so that they can be fixed into or on to the bearings box.

1. The snail cam (A) produces one event per revolution. Positioned on the shaft as a figure nine, facing the crank handle, it will only turn anticlockwise. Positioned as a six, it will turn only clockwise.
2. The four-lobed cam (B) produces four events per revolution, bobbing up and down. It can turn only clockwise.
3. The three-lobed cam (C) will work with a pin follower, but the bearing must not be too wide for the pin, or it will jam. A perspex shield, or any smooth-surfaced panel or bar, used as a guide against the block, will solve that problem.
4. The pear-shaped cam (D) produces an up and down motion with a dwell, or pause, period. For more than half the cycle the follower does not react. This is unlike the eccentric circular cam, which gives a continuous oscillating performance.
5. The oval cam (E) produces a similar action to the eccentric circular cam, but at twice the speed, providing two events per revolution.
6. The five-lobed cam (F), which gives a staccato up and down motion, can only work efficiently with a roller follower or a disc follower. A pin follower could jam on the lower parts of the radial surface. Only the roller can accurately and smoothly manage the peaks and troughs of the cam's profile, with the aid of a perspex shield.
7. The triangular cam (G) operates best with the roller follower. Those sharp little corners, unlike those of the three-lobed cam, would in time be dulled.

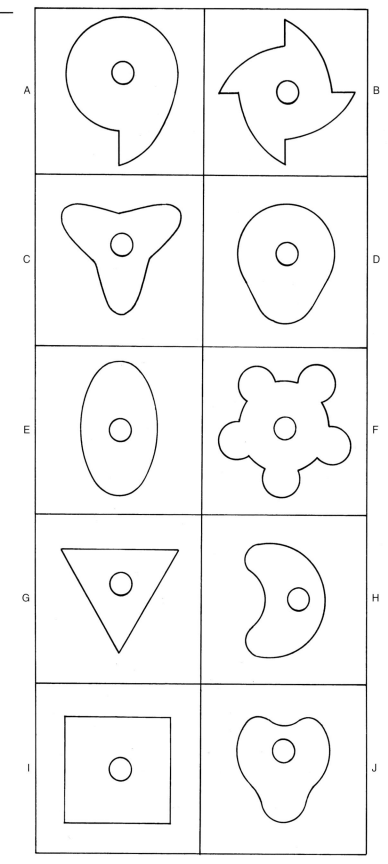

8. The crescent cam (H) produces a pleasing rhythmical and bouncy movement. It is important that the bearing for the roller follower is not too wide, or jamming will occur. Once again, a perspex shield would solve the problem.

9. The square cam (I) will actually work with a pin follower but, as with the triangular cam, it is a smoother ride with the roller, with less friction on the corner.

The central disc follower is fitted with a small dowel pin. It is checked from rotating too far by two other pins. The circular eccentric cam on the right lifts and rotates the outer edge of the disc follower, anti-clockwise.

The central disc follower is raised on its outer edge by the circular eccentric cam on the left, rotating clockwise. The mechanism serves as both cam and friction drive, moving the follower up and down and from side to side.

10. The radii of this cam (J) are dipped and raised as if bites have been taken out of the disc. The radial surface provides dwells in the action. It has a pretty movement, reminiscent of a trotting rider.

COLOUR AND NUMBER
THE CAMS

Working in Wood

The friction drive mechanism cannot be as efficient as a metal or plastic formed bevel gear, but for the purpose of making fairly simple automata and mechanical toys, the results can be perfectly adequate and satisfying, both aesthetically and mechanically. If a more positive performance than friction movement is required, pin wheels could help (*see* page 101, for details on gears), although they will take up more space in your design.

Working in wood is very different from working in metal. The tolerances are so much broader and the drill and the saw can 'drift' in wood. Use sharp drill bits and blades to counteract these negative forces. It is essential to test-drill bearings. If the hole is too generous, the follower may bob around like a cork at sea! One remedy is to wet the bearing, in order to shrink it. This trick is especially useful to tighten stops used at the end of shafts, if using friction fit. Conversely, to facilitate movement in a bearing, a little candle grease rubbed into it and on to the follower can reduce friction. Small party-cake candles are ideal for this.

In extreme temperature conditions, bearings can tighten, so pieces in storage should be insulated with bubble-wrap. A protective cardboard box will also help.

It may be necessary to use a panel of perspex or some other smooth-surfaced material to steady a follower in too wide a bearing. A horizontal bar placed against the top of the follower block will have the same stabilizing effect. If you can incorporate this ergonomically in your design, so much the better.

Wood is an imprecise material, and the amount of 'play' in a wooden bearing is critical. Even after test-drilling, the dowel

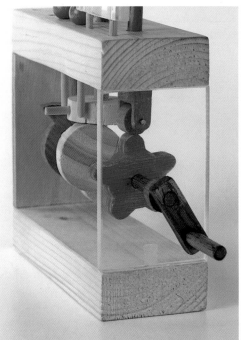

shaft of the follower in the bearing may not work 'on the night'. It is frustrating and you may be tempted to drill too wide a hole to allow ease of action. That can lead to problems, with the follower jamming on certain cams. Using a panel or bar, either openly or artfully concealed, can overcome these difficulties.

If your design does not allow for such problem-solving devices, remember that the deeper the follower's channel in the bearing, the better it will perform.

The Roller Follower

The free-running bearing or roller, fixed on the end of a pin follower, will facilitate tracking cams that have eventful profiles. An empirical approach will determine when and where you should use it. In most simple automata, it is rarely seen, because the cams are uncomplicated. It is only when the follower needs to track the cam's profile accurately that the device can play a useful role in relaying precisely the cam's message to the follower. It also reduces friction, which might be an important factor in the design of the piece.

Making Cams and Followers
1. Cut five discs A, from 1⅛in (28mm) dowel. Drill holes as indicated, to fit tightly on dowel rods. The middle three

The roller follower is at the lowest point on the profile of the pentagonal cam. There are five events per revolution, or cycle.

The roller is at the highest point on the profile of the pentagonal cam. The crank handle has moved from 20 to 25 past the hour, being one event in the cycle.

This roller is to be fixed to the end of a pin follower. It smoothes the path on a cam with an eventful profile.

PLAN 3
Making cams
and followers.

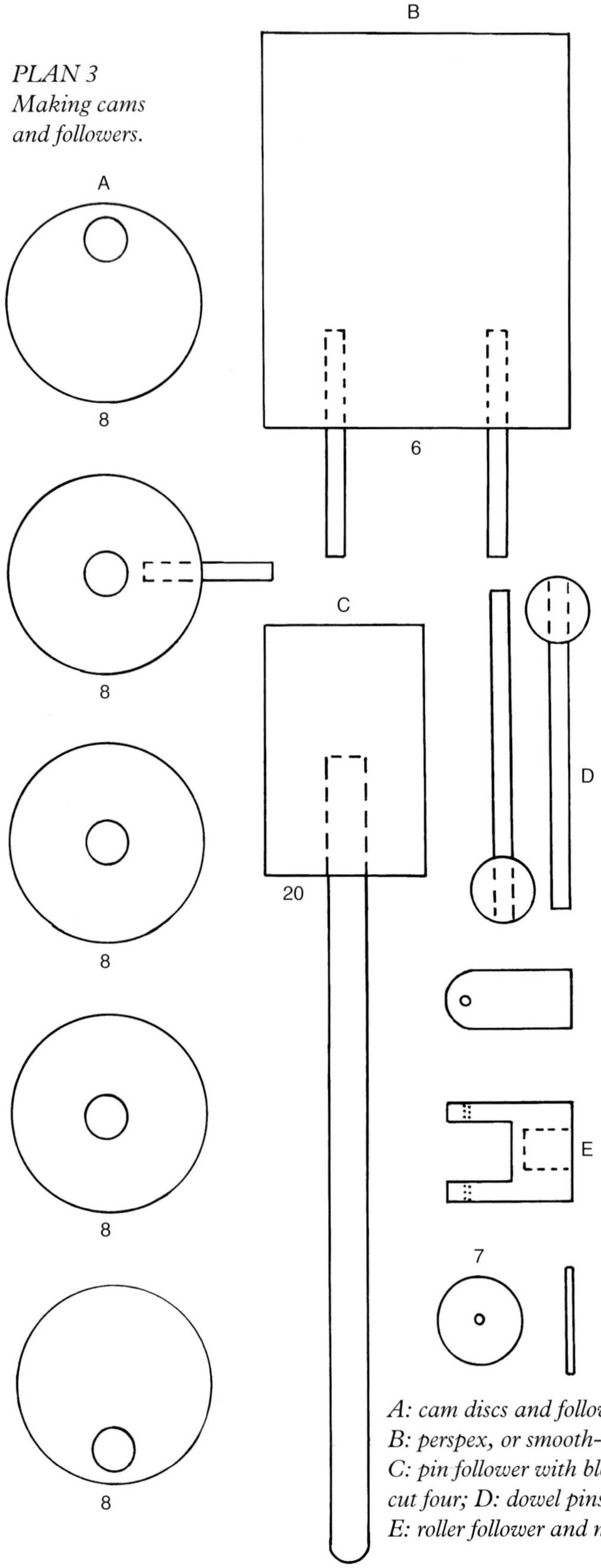

A: cam discs and followers;
B: perspex, or smooth-surfaced panel;
C: pin follower with block weight;
cut four; D: dowel pins and beads;
E: roller follower and mechanism.

are disc followers, one with a restraining pin to prevent it from swivelling too far. The outer two are eccentric cams, which fit on to the camshaft.

2. Cut a perspex or smooth-surfaced panel B. Drill holes in the base to receive the two small dowel pins.

3. Cut four large dowel pins, rounding their ends. Cut four blocks C, drilling central holes in their bases to fit on the dowel pins. These blocks are weights for the followers. One is stained green, one red, and two are plain. They fit into the bearings on top of the bearings box.

4. Cut five thin dowel pins 3mm ($\frac{1}{8}$in) as indicated. Drill a central hole in the side of the disc to receive the shortest pin. Fit the two shorter pins into the base of panel B. The longer dowel pins D fit into two small wooden beads. These are placed, vertically, in front of the central disc follower, with the pin, on top of the bearings box.

5. Assemble the roller follower E (*see the photo*). Drill a small central hole in the roller. A thin piece of piano wire, or a panel pin, cut to size, will serve as the pin that holds the roller in position. Drill the bearing before you cut out the central part of the device, in case it collapses. Ensure that the dowel roller fits, but not too snugly.

6. Colour and number the parts.

CRANKS

A crank can be a handle that turns a shaft or, indeed, a shaft that turns a handle. The crank pin, which plays such a major role in the making of automata, has a small 'handle' in the form of a pin fixed near the outer edge of the disc. This, when attached to a rod, moves it up and down and from side to side. The mechanism is known as the crank slider and has great versatility (*see* the three versions – slotted bearing, circular bearing and using pegs – in the photos opposite).

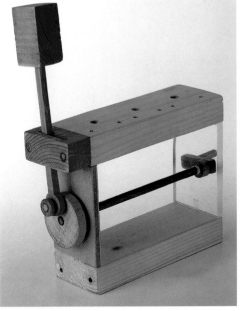

FAR LEFT: *The crankshaft turns the crank pin, which raises and lowers the weighted rod, backward and forward, within a fixed slotted bearing. This is called a crank slider.*

The crank has converted rotating motion into reciprocating motion. The amount of vertical movement can be seen.

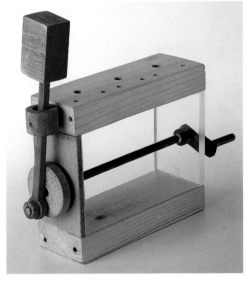

FAR LEFT: *The rod at its highest point is moving within a fixed circular bearing.*

There is less lateral movement in the circular bearing than in the slotted bearing.

In the slotted bearing version, in an open narrow box without a base, the rod rides, up and down, within the slot. It is a fairly vigorous, hammering movement.

The circular bearing version confines the lateral motion to a gentle nodding. The distance travelled and the height gained by the rod are exactly the same as with the slotted bearing. The amount of play within the circular bearing determines the degree of lateral action.

The third version of the crank slider allows for experimentation with the use of pegs. The lower the pegs are placed on the peg board, the greater the side-to-side movement. This version combines the actions offered by the other two and, at its most active, evokes the image of a boat bobbing

ABOVE: The crank slider allows sideways movement to increase when the pegs are fixed low, and to decrease when they are placed high.

ABOVE RIGHT: The movement suggests a boat bobbing up and down on the sea.

on the sea. This might be one example where a mechanism suggests an idea.

The common feature of these crank sliders is a rotating motion converted, by the crank, into a reciprocating motion. Although the rod moves vertically, the same distance for each version, it is the different types of bearing that govern side-to-side movements.

Making Crank Sliders

The following instructions are for making three types of crank slider to operate, separately, on the side panel H of the bearings box (*see* Plan 4, page 87).

1. Using ply or stripwood, drill a hole at the base of rod A. Cut out the rod, with the drilled hole, and chamfer the edges.
2. Cut the block B, and drill a hole in it to receive the top of rod A, which is, of course, square.
3. Cut out the peg board C and drill holes to accommodate 3mm (⅛in) dowel pins, and pegs D. The two pegs on the left, with wooden beads as heads, will fit into any of the central holes. The two pins on

the right are glued, flush with the surface, into the outer holes at the base of the peg board. This enables you to fix the board on to the side panel H, by inserting the pins into the two outer holes, at the top.

4. Cut out the disc E for the crank pin and drill holes as indicated. Cut and glue a dowel pin I, in the outer hole. Cut the dowel collet J for the crankshaft and drill a hole so that it will, by friction, fit on to the end. Cut a dowel washer K for the crankshaft and drill a large hole to fit loosely. The washer compensates for the thickness of the peg board and bearings. It enables rod A to work smoothly and straight, at 90 degrees.
5. Cut the circular bearing F, from ⅞in (22mm) dowel rod, or from ply, and drill a central hole in the side to receive 3mm (⅛in) dowel pins. Drill the large central hole, which is the bearing for rod A. Glue the dowel pin into position, ensuring that it does not encroach on the bearing's aperture. This little wooden 'O' fits, by friction, into the middle hole in the side panel H.
6. Cut the slotted bearings block G, with a guide slot for rod A to move in. This should be filed, if necessary, to ensure that there is enough, but not too much, play in the bearing. Drill 3mm (⅛in) holes to accommodate the dowel pins and glue them into the block. These must fit, by friction, into the outer holes at the top of the side panel H.

 COLOUR AND NUMBER THE PARTS

The Double Crankshaft

As with most rotating shafts, a crankshaft is supported by bearings at either end. Sometimes, if the shaft is long, more bearings in the middle may be required. Additional cranks can be added to the shaft, but they take up more space than cams. However, they do more powerful work.

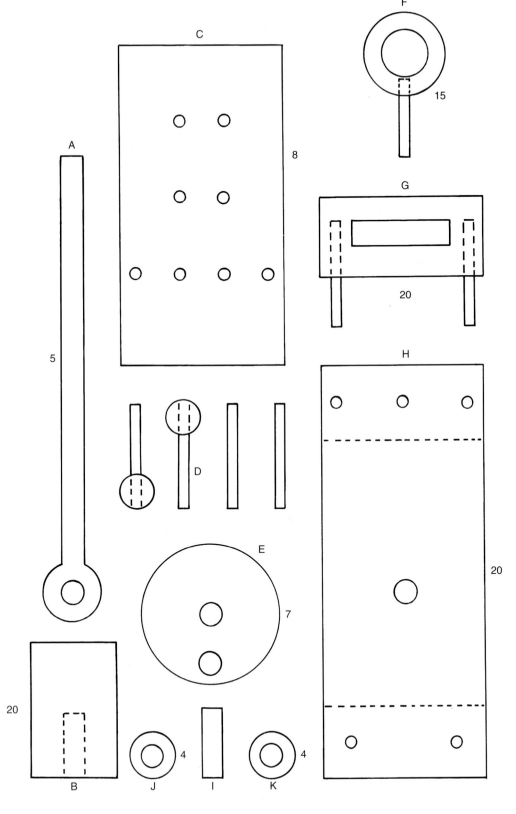

PLAN 4
Making crank sliders.
A: rod; B: block; C: peg
board; D: pegs; E: crank
disc; F: circular bearing
and peg; G: slotted bearing
and pegs; H: side panel; I:
dowel pin; J: dowel collet;
K: dowel washer.

As the red lever is down the crank beneath is up. While the blue lever is up, the crank below is down.

It can be seen that the crank merely follows the rotation of the handle. As the red lever is up the crank beneath is down. While the blue lever is down the crank below is up.

Strings or wires are looped loosely around the crank pins, to allow the pulling up and lowering of weighted levers. If the cranks are offset from each other they can operate in alternating rhythm.

The most important thing to remember in making crankshafts is that it is essential to determine the *throw* of a crank. This is the diameter of the path it travels in one revolution. Unless you allow for this, the mechanism may jam in the bearings box, or whatever device you employ to house the crankshaft. For example, the dimensions of the cranks in Plan 5 are not designed to work with front and back panels, since the box is open. With a closed box, the depth of the box would need to be wider, or the cranks smaller.

Making a Double Crankshaft
1. Cut a long dowel D, the complete length of the shaft on Plan 5. Cut two short dowels C, and one for the handle F.
2. Cut five lengths of 5×10mm ($\frac{3}{16} \times \frac{3}{8}$in) stripwood, as indicated, for the cranks B. Drill holes in them to accommodate dowels C, D and F.
3. Position the two cranks, as on the plan, with the shaft, as yet uncut, running through them with a tight friction fit. This is best done working on a grid, graph paper or calibrated cutting mat. It is important to build the crankshaft as truly square as possible. Acetate or cellophane are good materials to work on. They allow both transparency and protection of the grid's surface from excess glue.
4. Glue and insert the crank pins C into the top and bottom of the two cranks B, and the dowel handle F, into the remaining crank B.
5. The left-hand part of the shaft D (coloured red) can be glued into the cranks B. The blue part, however, must be left unglued and detachable to fit into the bearings box. A tight friction fit is essential here, as otherwise slippage could occur.
6. The handle assembly B/F is now glued to the shaft D, square to the cranks. When the crankshaft is completely dry, the two redundant parts that have been holding

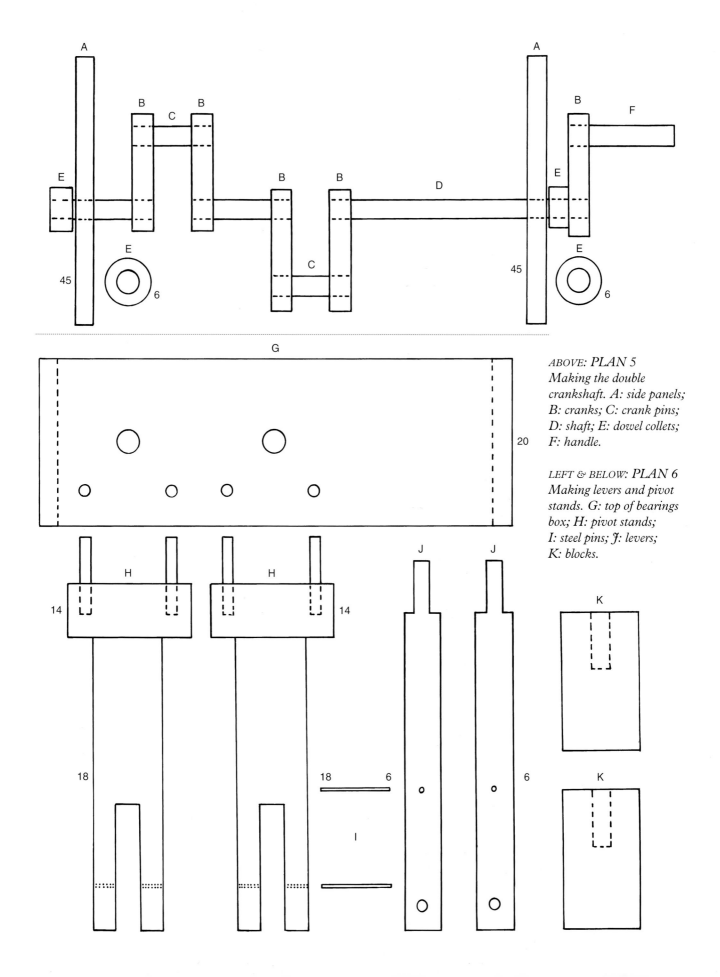

ABOVE: PLAN 5
Making the double
crankshaft. A: side panels;
B: cranks; C: crank pins;
D: shaft; E: dowel collets;
F: handle.

LEFT & BELOW: PLAN 6
Making levers and pivot
stands. G: top of bearings
box; H: pivot stands;
I: steel pins; J: levers;
K: blocks.

everything square are cut out. Strings or wires can now be looped loosely around the crank pins and fixed in position.

7. The two dowel collets E are cut from 12 × 6mm dowels and drilled to fit tightly on the shaft D. One is glued to support the handle assembly B/F, and the other serves as a tight friction stop for the end of the crankshaft.

To fit the crankshaft into the bearings box, insert the blue half through the bearing in the right side panel A. Put the red half through the bearing in the left side panel A, and join them together, inside the box.

COLOUR AND NUMBER
THE PARTS

Making Levers and Pivot Stands
The two pivot stands H are made in two parts, which are glued together and fitted, with pegs, into the top of the bearings box G. The weighted levers J/K are fixed by pins into the slots. Strings, attached to the crankshaft below, are passed through holes in the top of the bearings box G and tied to the ends of the levers J.

1. Cut the two pivot stands H, and drill central holes for the steel pins I, to friction fit. Cut out the slots and chamfer their edges.
2. Cut out the two plinths for the stands H, and drill holes to receive four 3mm (⅛in) dowel pins, which can be cut to length. These are inserted into the plinths to fit into the four smaller holes in the top of the bearings box G. Careful registration, in matching the pegs to the holes, is required.
3. Glue together the pivot stands and their plinths, as shown in Plan 6.
4. Cut out the levers J, and drill holes as indicated, one for the steel pin I, and the other for the string, which is to be tied to the ends of the levers J.

5. Cut out the two blocks K, and drill central holes in their bases to accommodate the square-ended shafts of the lever J. These square pegs can now be glued into the round holes.
6. Cut 2mm (1/16in) steel pins I, from piano wire, or use panel pins with their ends cut off and filed.
7. Place the weighted levers J/K into their slots in the pivot stands H. Push the steel pins I through the channels, to friction fit. They should work freely within their slots.
8. With the complete assembly in position and the crankshaft in the bearings box G, feed the strings through the large holes in the top G. Loosely tie the strings to the ends of the levers J, and test the alternating movement. If there were no intention to dismantle the mechanism, glue would be dabbed on the knots.

LINKAGE MECHANISMS

A linkage can be made from a crank, a lever or a connecting rod. It transfers movement from one mechanical part to another, changing its direction or the amount of movement. It can even change the way it moves … or do all these things at once!

Making a Linkage Mechanism
1. The bars and levers can be cut from either 4mm ply or stripwood.
2. Before cutting out the linkage bar A, drill holes in it as indicated on Plan 7. This is easier and more accurate than drilling a large hole in a small piece, which might move in the drilling process.
3. Cut two long dowel pins B, 3mm (⅛in), and cut and drill holes in the dowel collets C.
4. Drill holes and cut out the fixed bar E. Glue the two long dowel pins B, flush with its surface. These, when the mechanism is assembled, are to fit into the two outer holes at the top of the side panel of the bearings box.

FAR LEFT: When the crank pin rotates, the linkage bar to which it is attached transfers movement to the vertical lever pivoting on the fixed bar.

The rotary motion of the linkage bar turns into a side-to-side movement of the vertical lever. Half a turn will thrust it forward, and a complete turn will draw it back.

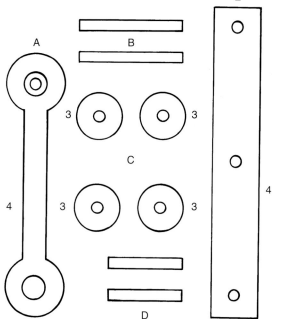
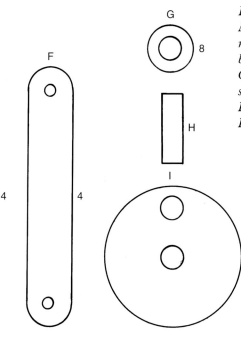

PLAN 7
Making a linkage mechanism. A: linkage bar; B: dowel pins; C: dowel collets; D: dowel spindles; E: fixed bar; F: lever; G: dowel collet; H/I: crank disc and pin.

5. Drill holes in, and cut out, the lever F.
6. Cut the crank pin disc I, from either dowel or ply. Drill holes as indicated, cut and glue the dowel pin H into the outer hole.
7. Cut the two short dowel spindles D, 3mm (⅛in), and insert one of them, freely, through the vacant hole in the fixed bar E. Secure this with a tight dowel collet C, adjacent to the two long, projecting dowel pins B, in the fixed bar E.
8. Place one end of the lever F on to the spindle D, and secure this joint with a tight dowel collet C.
9. Place the linkage bar A on top of the lever G, inserting a dowel spindle D through them both. Lock the spindle at either end with tight dowel collets C, ensuring that the parts move freely.

10. To assemble the mechanism, insert the fixed bar E, with the two dowel pins, into the side panel of the bearings box. This should have holes, already drilled, to receive the pins, as in Plan 1B. Fix the crank pin tightly on to the shaft, attaching the linkage bar A to it and sealing it with dowel collet G.

COLOUR AND NUMBER THE PARTS

The Four-Bar Linkage Mechanism

Also known as the quadratic-crank mechanism, the four-bar linkage mechanism is also sometimes referred to as the three-bar linkage, since only three bars are visible. The fourth is an invisible, stationary bar, which connects the lever in the pivot block to the crank.

Whether three- or four-bar, the mechanism consists of four links connected by pin joints; the first link has already been mentioned; the second link is the crank; the third is the coupler, which connects the crank, or linkage bar, to the fourth link, which is the lever.

The linkage employs a crank slider device (*see* page 86), with pegs to contain the linkage bar. The bar can make a complete revolution while the lever moves from side to side, translating rotation into oscillation.

Making the Four-Bar Linkage Mechanism
Unlike the previous mechanisms, the four-bar linkage needs an extension of the dimensions afforded by the bearings box; in short, it requires a plinth.

1. Cut out the plinth A, as shown on Plan 8. Now refer to Plan 1C, which shows the location of peg holes in the base of the bearings box. Cut the four pegs to fit. Drill four corresponding holes in the plinth A. Glue and insert the pegs, so that the two nearest the large holes in the plinth, to be used later on, protrude 5mm (³⁄₁₆in) and the other two protrude 14mm (⁹⁄₁₆in).
2. Cut out the linkage bar B, the coupler C, and the lever D. Drill holes, as indicated.
3. Cut out the base E for the pivot block F. Locate and drill holes for the two dowel pegs, which are cut to length. These fit into plinth A, as shown by the dotted lines.
4. Cut out pivot block F, and drill a hole to receive the block pin I. Now cut out the recess in the block. Glue this to its base E, as shown on the plan. They can now be glued into the block E.

Four-bar linkage consists of four links connected by pin joints. Rotation of the crank is translated into an oscillating movement of the lever, by means of the coupler bar that connects them.

FAR RIGHT: The crank's action turns into an ellipse where the linkage bar meets the coupler. It then turns into an arc, where the coupler joins the lever.

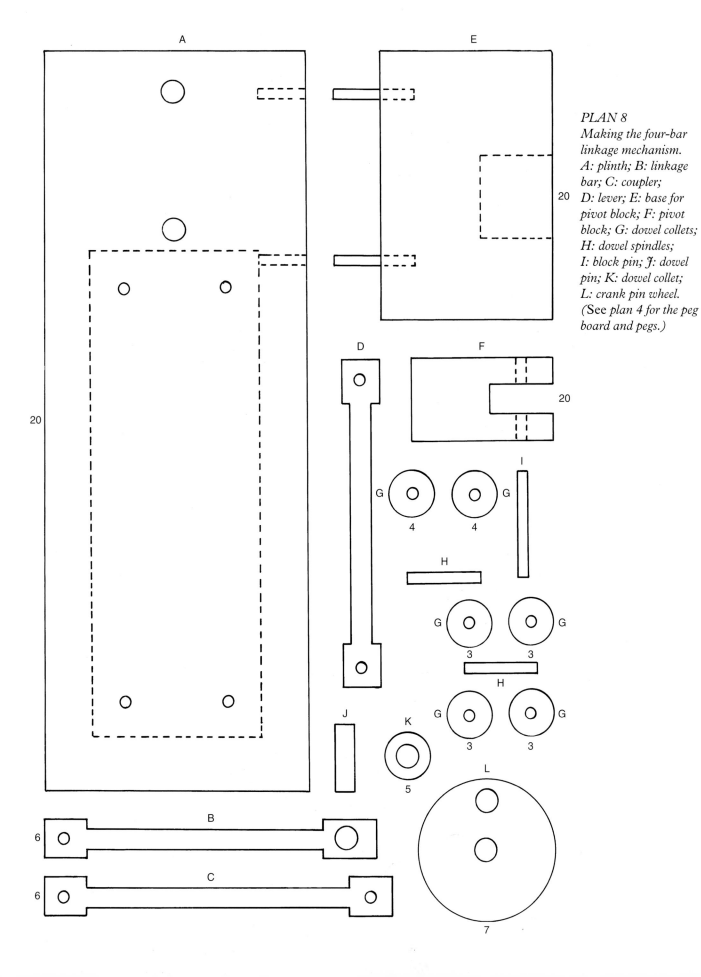

PLAN 8
*Making the four-bar linkage mechanism.
A: plinth; B: linkage bar; C: coupler; D: lever; E: base for pivot block; F: pivot block; G: dowel collets; H: dowel spindles; I: block pin; J: dowel pin; K: dowel collet; L: crank pin wheel. (See plan 4 for the peg board and pegs.)*

5. Cut six dowel collets G and two dowel spindles H. Cut a longer dowel for the block pin I.

6. Cut the crank pin dowel J, the dowel collet K, and the wheel itself L.

7. To assemble the mechanism, slot the pivot block E/F into the plinth A, as shown, with the two fixed pegs. Insert the crankshaft through the bearings box and fix the crank pin J/L to its end. Press the bearings box on to the pegs in the plinth A.

8. Refer to Plan 4C. The crank slider peg board and pegs are essential to the operation of the four-bar linkage. This should have been cut and drilled already if you are working, in sequence, through the mechanisms. Fix the peg board, by

the glued-in pegs, into the outer holes in the side of the bearings box.

9. Assemble the three bars B, C and D. The linkage bar B is fixed under the coupler D, loosely locked by a spindle H and two collets G. The lever D attaches likewise to the other end of the coupler C. Glue the collets to the spindles but ensure that the three-pieced mechanism works freely within the joints.

10. Fix the free end of the linkage bar B on to the crank pin J/L. Place the two-headed dowel pins into the peg board (made from Plan 4), to govern the linkage bar B.

11. Insert the free end of the lever D into the pivot block F, passing the block pin I through and securing with dowel collets K. Leave one of these unglued, so that the mechanism can be dismantled.

 COLOUR AND NUMBER THE PARTS

The Bell Crank

This linkage is actually a kind of lever. If the L-shaped component is extended, in either direction, the movement achieved gives greater leverage. This can also be done by moving the position of the fulcrum; some patient experimentation should bring about satisfying results when incorporating this linkage into a piece. One action the movement seems to evoke is that of a woodpecker.

Making the Bell Crank

1. Cut the lever support block A, from $^{13}/_{16}$in (20mm) batten, and drill a hole, as indicated on Plan 9, to a depth of 16mm ($^{5}/_{8}$in).

2. Cut out the extension block D. Drill a hole to match the hole in the lever support block A, to a depth of 17mm ($^{11}/_{16}$in).

3. Cut the thick dowel pin C to fit into both these holes. Glue it into the lever support block A.

The bell crank linkage alters an up-and-down motion into a side-to-side motion. This is achieved by the L-shaped component joining the linkage bar to the lever, at the top.

The horizontal, push-pull action of the lever, at the top, moves 25mm (1in) on this model.

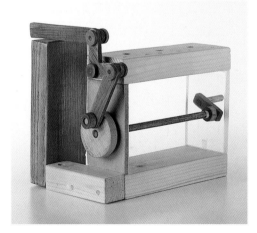

Making the bell crank. A: lever support block;
B: dowel spindles; C: dowel pin; D: extension
block; E: dowel collets; F: lever; G: L-shaped
arm; H/I: pivot pin; J: linkage bar; K: dowel
collet; L/M: crank pin; N: washer.

4. Cut two thin dowel pins to fit holes that you now drill into the side of the extension block D.
5. Cut out the lever F, and drill a hole, as shown, in one end. Cut out the L-shaped arm G, drilling three holes where indicated. Now cut the linkage bar J, drilling a small and larger hole.
6. Cut out the dowel spindles B, and four dowel collets E.
7. To assemble the bell crank, place the linkage bar J over the bottom of the L-shaped arm G. Insert a dowel spindle D through the two holes and secure with two dowel collets E at either end.
8. Now do the same for the lever F, where it meets the top of the L-shaped arm G. Glue the two pairs of collets E to their spindles B, ensuring that the mechanism moves freely within the joints.
9. To attach the mechanism to the side panel of the bearings box, first insert the crankshaft and slip the washer N on to the end. Then fix the crank pin L/M next to the washer N.
10. Fix the linkage bar J on to the crank pin L/M, and friction fit the thick dowel collet K on to the pin.
11. Insert the pivot pin H/I through the centre hole of the L-shaped arm G, and halfway into the central hole in the top side of the bearings box. Centre the mechanism over the crank pin L/M. Pushing it right home will impair the movement.
12. Push the extension block D, with the fixed pins, into the base of the bearings box, where two holes are located on the side.

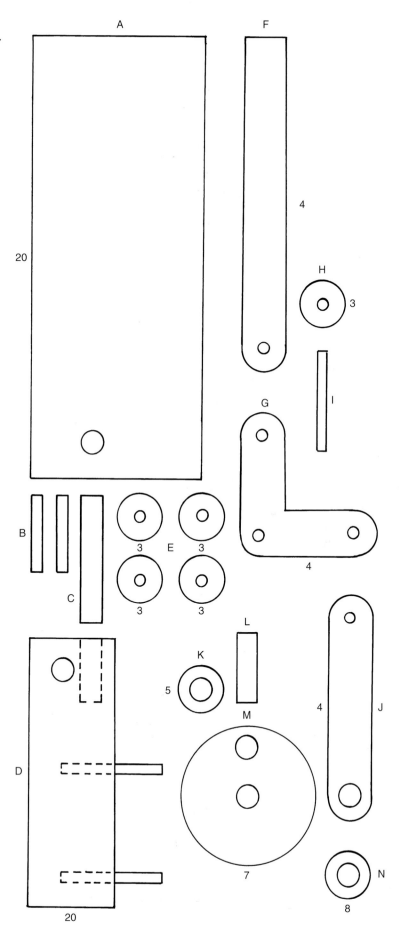

The ratchet is a notched wheel, enabling movement to be effected in one direction only. This is achieved by a driving pawl pushing the ratchet wheel forward and a supplementary pawl checking it from slipping back.

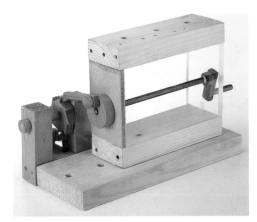

The ratchet block assembly shows the supplementary pawl, supported by a spring, engaging the ratchet wheel. This moves forward one notch per revolution.

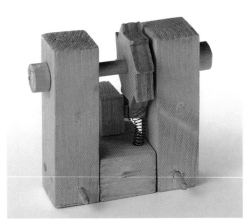

ABOVE: *Detail showing how the supplementary pawl is positioned on the block. The spring is super-glued into holes in the block and the underside of the pawl.*

The driving pawl, the crank pin and the dowel collet, which locks it in position.

13. Insert the lever support block A, and its fixed dowel pin C, into the extension block D. Place the lever A on top and operate.

COLOUR AND NUMBER THE PARTS

RATCHETS

The ratchet supplies movement that is not continuous and can give a piece more time in which to complete a cycle. This intermittent, or stepped motion is governed by the number of teeth on the ratchet wheel.

On this model there are eight teeth on the wheel. In order to complete the whole cycle, the crank needs to be turned eight times, with one revolution moving the ratchet wheel forward one notch. At, say, a second at a time, one cycle takes eight seconds.

The ratchet mechanism is governed by a long arm, the driving pawl, which turns on the crank pin, pushing the notched wheel forward. Below the wheel is a shorter arm, the supplementary pawl, which ensures that the wheel stops at the right place, correctly positioned for each push of the driving pawl.

Making the Ratchet Assembly
1. Cut out two pillars A, and drill holes in them, as indicated on Plan 10. Drill holes in their sides, centrally positioned, to receive two cut 3mm (⅛in) dowels. Glue these in.
2. Cut out the ratchet block B/C. Drill a shallow – 3mm (⅛in) – hole in block B, for the spring D. The exact diameter must be determined by the size of spring inserted.
3. Drill holes in the sides of block B to match the holes you cut in the pillars A. Cut and insert 3mm (⅛in) dowel pins to fit them.

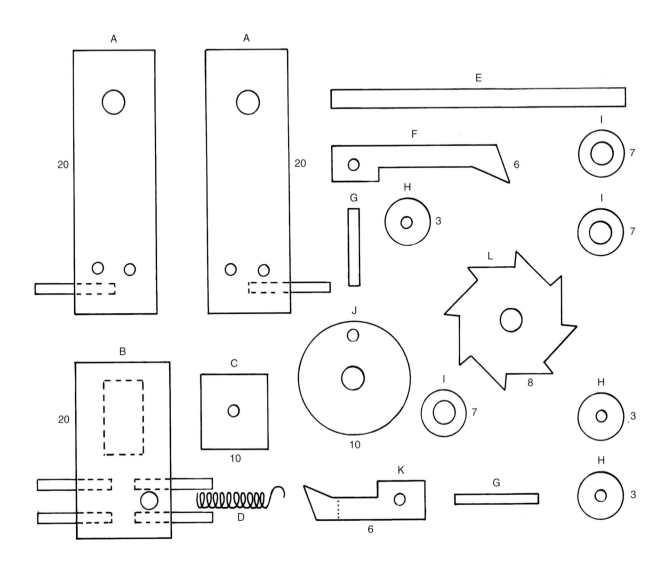

4. Drill a hole through the small block C, position it as indicated by the dotted line, and glue it on to block B.

5. Fit one end of the spring D into the shallow hole in block B. Fix it with superglue. Straighten out the other end of the spring D 10mm (⅜in) long with pliers.

6. Cut out the supplementary pawl K. Drill a narrow channel through it, as indicated by the dotted line. Also drill a hole in it for a dowel spindle G, cut to length.

7. Insert the 10mm (⅜in) straightened piece of wire at the end of the spring D through the narrow channel in the foot of the supplementary pawl K.

8. Cut a dowel spindle G. Insert it through block C, and the supplementary pawl K.

9. Cut two dowel collets H, glueing one end to the spindle G, and friction fitting the other end to lock the pawl K, in position.

10. Cut to length the dowel shaft E. Cut out the driving pawl F. Cut and drill two thick shaft collets I and a thin collet H.

11. Cut the crank and pin J/G, and lastly the ratchet wheel L.

PLAN 10
Making the ratchet assembly. A: pillars; B/C: ratchet block; D: spring; E: dowel shaft; F: driving pawl; G: dowel spindle; H: dowel collets; I: shaft collets; J/G: crank and pin; K: supplementary pawl; L: ratchet wheel. (See Plan 8 for plinth.)

Arranging the Ratchet Assembly

1. Slot the two pillars A on to the dowel pins, each side of the ratchet block B, which has been assembled already.
2. Insert the dowel shaft E through one of the pillars A, and the ratchet wheel L. Pass it through the other pillar A. Secure it with thick shaft collets I at either end. Ensure that the ratchet wheel is directly over the supplementary pawl K on the ratchet block, B/C.
3. Refer to Plan 8A, which shows how to make the plinth for the bearings box, which fits on to the plinth pegs. Insert the crankshaft into the bearings box and friction fit the crank pin J/G on to the end.
4. Fit the driving pawl, loosely, on the pin. Secure with a shaft collet I.
5. Push the ratchet block B/C, with its two protruding pins, into the side of the plinth, as indicated on Plan 8A.
6. Place the driving pawl F on to the ratchet wheel L. Turn the crank handle clockwise or anti-clockwise, but the wheel will only go forwards.

COLOUR AND NUMBER
THE PARTS

The Geneva Wheel, while not strictly a ratchet, does provide intermittent, or stepped motion. Unlike the ratchet, the wheel can turn in either direction, but without the ratchet's locking mechanism. It is shown here without its shield, which can be seen on the plan.

The Geneva Wheel

Known by watchmakers as the Geneva Stop, this mechanism works like a film projector, stepping the film on, one frame at a time. The crank pin enters each channel, or slot, at every full turn, so it takes four turns to complete the cycle. The advantage of this is that it provides a long pause, or dwell period between each event.

Making the Geneva Wheel

1. Cut out the cross A, and drill a central hole, as indicated on Plan 11.
2. Cut the shield B (shown on the plan as a dotted line), and drill the hole.
3. Cut out the crank wheel C, and drill two holes.
4. Cut the dowel pin D, the dowel collet E, and the dowel pin F.
5. To assemble the mechanism, insert the crankshaft into the bearings box.
6. Glue the shield B on to the crank wheel C, so that the holes line up.
7. Glue the dowel pin F into the top hole in the crank wheel C.
8. Glue the dowel collet E on to the end of the spindle D.
9. Insert the spindle and collet D/E through the hole in the cross A, to friction fit.
10. Insert the assembled Geneva Wheel into the middle hole in the top, side, of the bearings box.
11. Locate the pin F of the crank wheel into one of the four slots, or channels, in the cross A.
12. Operate either clockwise or anti-clockwise and the Geneva Wheel will turn in the opposite direction.

COLOUR AND NUMBER
THE PARTS

DRIVES

The standards and tolerances found in 'grown-up' engineering do not apply to most modern automatists. Their work,

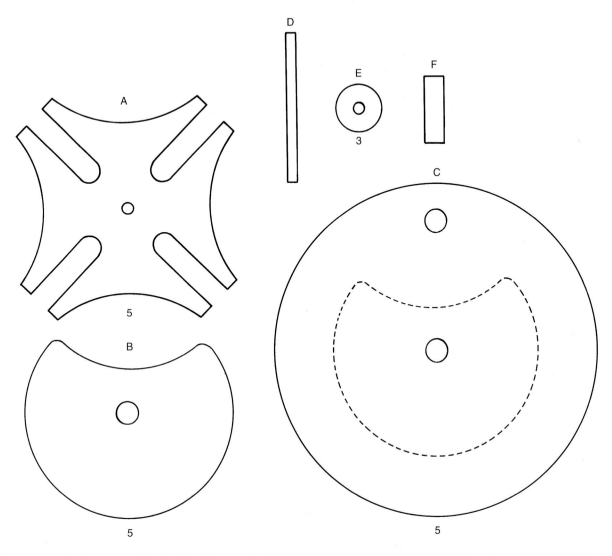

while being highly creative and inspirational is, for the most part, uncomplicated, providing pretty basic mechanical movements. With this low-tech approach in mind, it is possible to turn to the model shop to minimize the tedium of making certain component parts. Making your own pulleys and drive wheels from wood is simple enough, but the world of toothed drive belts and tensioning is beyond the scope of this book.

Positive and Friction Drives

There are two types of drive: positive and friction. A chain and sprocket system is positive, always in synchronization, because the

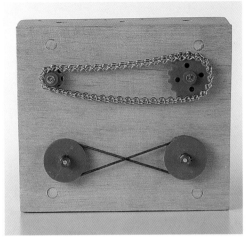

ABOVE: PLAN 11
Making the Geneva Wheel. A: cross; B: shield; C: crank wheel; D: dowel spindle; E: dowel collet; F: dowel pin.

Positive and friction drives are obtainable from model shops. They serve well enough, hidden inside a piece but, aesthetically, leave something to be desired.

teeth of the wheel are permanently locked into the links of the chain. Friction drive is a much freer affair, where there is slippage and, therefore, a less accurate transmission of the rotary connection.

The type of drive used depends on how exact the performance needs to be. If it is vital for an action to be repeated with absolute regularity, then a chain and sprocket system should be used. If, on the other hand, it does not much matter that the drive band slips a little, losing accuracy, then friction drive is the way to go. One advantage of friction drive is that the flexible metal drive band can be crossed over and the action of the driven wheel reversed.

Whether you use a positive chain and sprocket system, or a friction drive band with pulleys, you may need to calculate speed differences between the driven wheel and the driver. With pulleys, use the diameter of the wheels; with the sprocket system, count the number of teeth. For instance, in the example here, the number of teeth on the driver sprocket is eight, and the driven sprocket has sixteen. Since the pulleys for the friction drive band are of the same size they will, naturally, rotate at the same speed. If they are twisted, they will turn in opposite directions.

GEARS

Gear wheels are really like little levers, meshed, to provide continuous action. They allow some components to move more slowly, or faster and more powerfully than others. As with drive wheels, this can be achieved by either the positive method, locking the cogs into each other, or by friction discs, with gravity supplying the magic.

Making simple automata and mechanical toys involves only the most modest of gearing methods, whether they use tooth-driven wheels or friction-driven discs. Gears, like chain and sprocket wheels and pulleys, can be bought from model shops; while they work very efficiently, they are rather unlovely to behold, so tuck them away well out of sight if you do use them.

Wooden cut cogwheels are another matter. All that precise cutting can be justifiably flaunted. Many modern automatists, unlike their predecessors, like to show the workings and reveal the magic. On the other hand, not all pieces lend themselves to this approach and there is something to be said for hiding the mechanics, especially if you believe that, by revealing them, you diminish the wizardry. Each maker needs to decide whether to be a magician or engineer. Or both.

Making Cogwheels
Make the painstaking cutting of wooden cogwheels much easier by laying out wooden struts, evenly spaced, on a disc covered by another disc, and glueing them

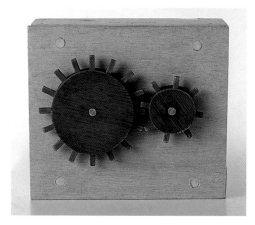

The small pinion wheel has half the number of teeth as the larger, driven wheel. As the pinion turns clockwise, the larger wheel rotates anti-clockwise, and at half the speed.

An alternative, effective and easier method of making cogwheels is to use wooden struts. These are glued, sandwiched between two discs.

7. To make the cogwheels G and H, cut out and drill as shown on the plan.
8. Insert the two rivets F, with washers E between the work and the wheels.
9. Cut a plywood backboard 127 × 108 × 5mm (5 × 4¼ × ³⁄₁₆in). Position the wheels as on the plan.

COLOUR AND NUMBER THE PARTS

Pin Wheels

To construct a pair of pin wheels, first draw two circles, the size to be determined by the ratio you choose. To use the ratio shown here, which is two to one, draw circles with a two to one ratio in their diameters, for example, 80mm and 40mm. These measurements are the diameters of the pitch circles on which the pins are located. The perimeter should extend beyond the pitch circles, to accommodate the pins, with a 7mm strip for the larger disc and 6mm strip for the small disc. The diameters of the cut circles will now measure 94mm and 52mm, respectively.

The pitch circles are divided up so that the number of pins are in the same ratio. Here, there are 24 pins on the large disc

Detail of the simple construction of the strutted cogwheel.

together. The action is the same for both methods, which require careful testing of the relative positions of the bearings. Ensure that both wheels move easily, forwards and backwards.

Making Gearwheels
1. To make the strutted wheels, cut and drill two small discs A, as indicated on Plan 12 (*see* page 102).
2. Cut eight small struts B to size, and glue on to the small disc A.
3. Cut and drill two large discs C.
4. Cut 16 struts to size and glue in position on the large disc C, as shown.
5. Glue disc A on to small strut B, inserting a rivet F through the two small discs A.
6. Glue disc C on to the large struts D, inserting a rivet F through the two large discs C.

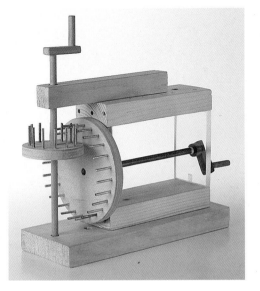

Pin wheels give a positive drive in both directions, serving as surrogate bevel gears. The two wheels mesh at an angle of 45 degrees, so that the rotary plane is changed from vertical to horizontal, or vice versa.

PLAN 12
Making gearwheels.
A: small disc; B: small
struts; C: large disc; D:
large struts; E: washer;
F: rivet; G: large cogwheel;
H: small pinion wheel;
I: plywood backboard (not
illustrated) 127 × 108 ×
5mm (5 × 4¼ × ³⁄₁₆in).

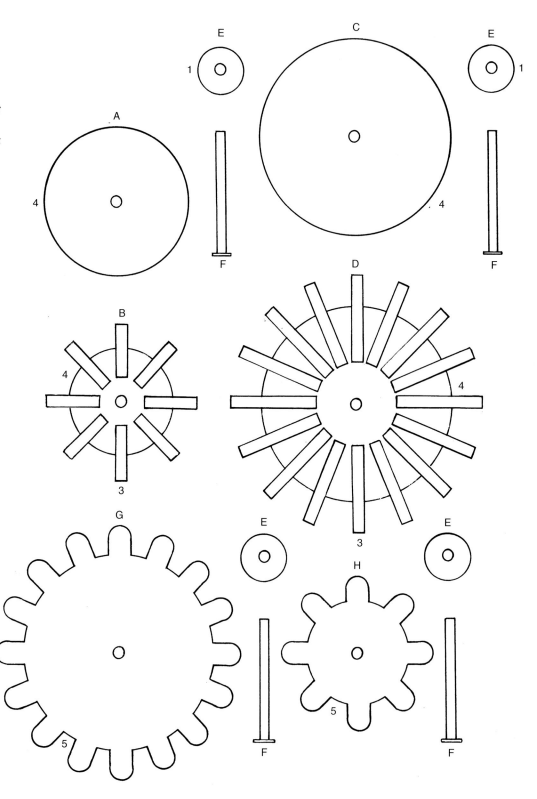

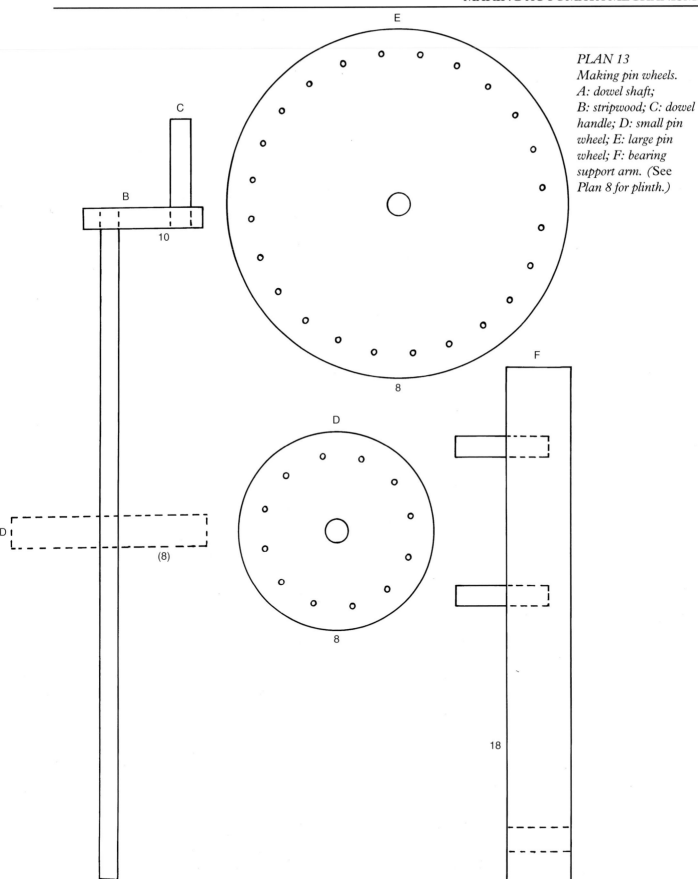

E

C

B

10

PLAN 13
Making pin wheels.
A: dowel shaft;
B: stripwood; C: dowel
handle; D: small pin
wheel; E: large pin
wheel; F: bearing
support arm. (See
Plan 8 for plinth.)

F

8

D

(8)

D

8

18

A

and 12 on the small one. To ascertain the angles for the division of the circles, divide 360 by the number of pins (24). That gives 15 segments for the large disc; 360 divided by the number of pins (12) gives 30 segments for the small disc.

As long as the ratios are kept compatible, the pin wheels will work. Computer software designed for drawing may make life a little easier, but it can be done with a compass, dividers and a protractor.

Panel pins, with their heads snipped off and filed, are used for the pin wheels. To mark the pins for cutting, wrap 12mm tape around them as a guide for snipping. A spirit marking pen could also be used if you wish to sand off the heads to a smooth finish.

Making Pin Wheels
1. Cut the dowel shaft A, as indicated on Plan 13.
2. Cut and drill holes in 5 × 10mm stripwood B.
3. Cut the dowel handle C, and glue into stripwood B.
4. Cut the small pin wheel D. Drill one central hole for the dowel shaft A, and 12 small holes, as shown, in which to friction fit panel pins.
5. Cut the large pin wheel E. Drill one central hole for the crank shaft and 24 small holes in which to friction fit panel pins.
6. Hammer in 12 panel pins to friction fit into the small pin wheel D, so that 12mm (½in) protrudes from the surface when they are cut and filed.
7. Do the same with 24 pins for the large pin wheel E.
8. Cut out the bearing support F. Drill holes for the two dowel pegs, as shown, not all the way through.
9. Cut the two dowel pegs and glue them into the bearing support arm F.
10. Drill a bearing hole for the shaft in the bearing support arm F, sufficient to allow the dowel shaft B to rotate freely.

Assembling the Pin Wheels
1. Insert the crank shaft into the bearing box, and fit it on to the plinth, with peg holes, from Plan 8.
2. Fit the large pin wheel E on to the end of the crankshaft.
3. Glue the dowel shaft A into the small pin wheel D, halfway up, as shown on the plan.
4. Insert the bottom of the dowel shaft A into the outer hole drilled in the plinth.
5. Insert the top end of the dowel shaft A through the bearing in the bearing support arm F. Press the two pegs into the holes in the top of the bearings box, nearest the pin wheels D and E.
6. Friction fit the dowel handle C on to the end of the vertical dowel shaft A. Leave it unglued, so that it can be dismantled.
7. Operate the mechanism, using either horizontal or vertical crank handles, clockwise and anti-clockwise.

 COLOUR AND NUMBER THE PARTS

The Friction-Driven Pole

After the cam, this is probably the most popular mechanism in making simple automata. The plane of rotation is turned from horizontal to vertical movement, just like the pin wheel. However, unlike the positive meshing of pins afforded by that device, these discs rely on friction and gravity for their power. In short, what they gain in simplicity, they lose in accuracy. Fortunately, accuracy is not always a prerequisite of performance.

The lower disc turns the upper disc because of its location under its outer edge. Friction supplies the movement and gravity ensures that the discs stay in contact.

Making the Friction-Driven Pole
1. Cut out the support block A. Drill two holes in the base to receive dowel pegs, as shown on Plan 8. These must be

compatible with the two holes in the plinth on Plan 8.

2. Cut the dowel pole D. Fix and glue a wooden bead to the top, widening the hole as necessary.

3. Drill a hole in the top of the support block A, to receive the dowel pole D, so that it can easily rotate in the hole.

4. Cut the dowel pegs and insert them into the support block A, as shown. Ensure that these will fit into the holes in the plinth, from Plan 8.

5. Cut the driver disc B, and drill a central hole to receive the dowel pole D. Glue in place.

6. Glue the driven disc C to the lower part of the dowel pole D, as indicated.

7. To assemble the mechanism, insert the crankshaft into the bearings box and fit it on to the plinth with pegs (from Plan 8).

8. Fix the driver disc B on to the end of the crankshaft.

9. Locate the pegs of the support block A, and insert into the holes in the plinth.

10. Place the dowel pole D into the hole in the support block A, so that it rests on the driver disc B.

11. Operate the mechanism in either direction.

COLOUR AND NUMBER
THE PARTS

LEVERS

The lever was probably the first mechanism invented by man. Although the wheel may have been accorded greater importance in the subsequent development of machinery, it almost certainly owes its invention to a prehistoric being using a club as a lever to dislodge a boulder, which hurtled downhill and thus planted the idea. Later generations added refinements to the axle, developed spokes and, subsequently, cogs and cams, and even hubcaps.

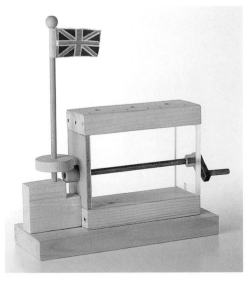

The friction-driven pole performs the same action as the pin wheel, but with half the complexity, and accuracy. It relies on friction and gravity to rotate, rather than the positive meshing of pins.

BELOW: PLAN 14
Making the friction-driven pole.
A: support block; B: driver disc; C: driven disc; D: dowel pole. (See Plan 8 for plinth.)

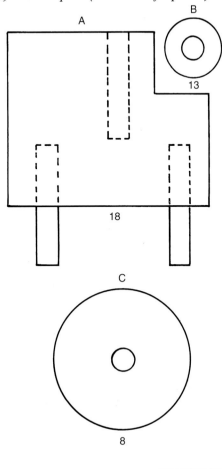

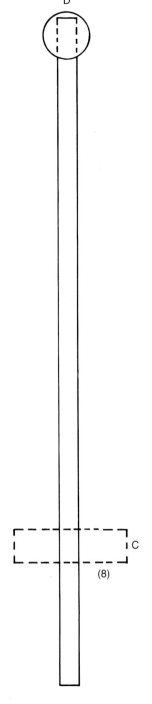

As the crankshaft turns, the crank pin lifts and drops the lever through a small arc.

FAR RIGHT: If the motion is too fast, the lever could fly off the crank pin unless it is locked by a pivot block, as it is here.

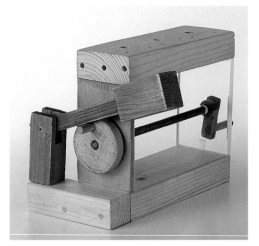

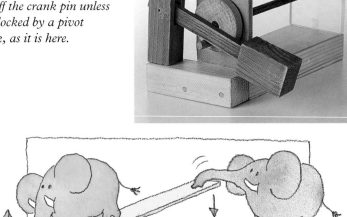

A lever of the first order has the fulcrum located between the effort and the load, as in a pair of pliers. A lever of the second order has the load between the fulcrum and the effort, as in a wheelbarrow. A lever of the third order has the effort applied between the fulcrum and the load. Tweezers are an example.

There is a great deal of theory pertaining to levers, but much of it has limited relevance to the building of automata. The best approach for a maker of automata is to keep it simple. (For those who wish to delve deeper, there are many books on the subject.) A basic acquaintance with the lever and its functions is necessary, however; the 'Elephants' Effort' illustrations left should serve to explain the three classes of lever. The pink elephants are the loads. The blue elephants supply the effort. The fulcrums are the pivot points upon which the plank rests.

It was Archimedes ('Give me a fulcrum on which to rest and I will move the earth!') who devised the system of dividing levers into three different orders. All levers fall into the three classes. They can be used separately, like a spanner; in pairs, like scissors; or connected together, like lazy tongs. They can even be used in multiples, as in the teeth of a cogwheel, which are really a series of tiny levers lifting other levers. Most levers fall into the first and second classes, because they give a mechanical advantage, moving a *large load* using *small effort*. The third type is more unusual because its mechanical advantage is negligible. Indeed, the force needed to use it is greater than the force it can move.

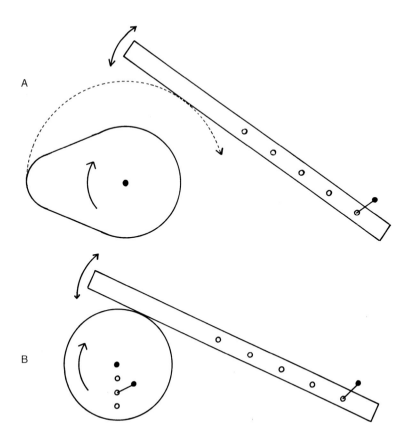

ABOVE: Testing levers can be simply done by using cut-out card and pins. A shows a pear-shaped cam, which produces much the same performance for the lever as B, the eccentric disc, does for its lever. By experimenting with the pin holes, you can quickly and cheaply test the best positions for your mechanism.

ABOVE RIGHT: The slotted lever's positive contact with the crank pin does not depend on gravity, but moves within its restricted channel.

Restricted and Unrestricted Levers

The essential thing to remember when making levers is to construct their pivot points so that when the piece is moved or handled, the levers do not fall out of position. If you are using a pivot block in which to house the lever, ensure that the slot is deep enough to allow freedom of action, but not so deep that it does not act as a stop to prevent the lever from flying off the crank pin.

The advantage of the restricted, slotted lever is that, with or without a pivot block,

the path of the lever is always controlled within its channel.

Making Slotted and Plain Levers
1. Cut out the lever support block A, from 20mm (¹³⁄₁₆in) batten, and drill holes as indicated on Plan 15.
2. Cut two thin dowel pins and glue these into the two small holes in the lever support block A.
3. Cut out the short pivot block B. Drill holes for the support peg and spindle I. Cut out the slot for the lever.

The performance is similar to the crankshaft's string-operated 'nodding donkey', although here it is driven within its restricted limit.

PLAN 15
Making slotted and plain
levers. A: lever support
block; B: short pivot block;
C: slotted lever; D: tall
pivot block; E: plain lever;
F/G: crank and pin;
H: blocks; I: spindles.

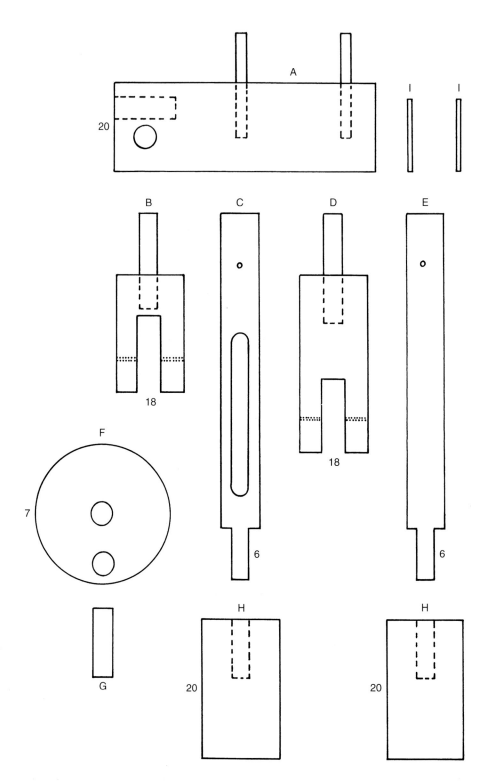

4. Cut the dowel support peg and glue it into the hole in the support block A.

5. Repeat Step 3 for the tall pivot block D.

6. Cut out the slot first in the slotted lever C, and then the lever itself. Drill a hole to receive the spindle I.

7. Cut out the plain lever E, and drill a hole in it for the spindle I, which you now cut from ¹⁄₁₆in (1.6mm) piano wire (or use a panel pin).

8. Cut out and drill the crank and pin F/G. Insert and glue the dowel pin into the outer hole in the crank wheel.

9. Cut out the blocks H, drilling holes to receive the ends of the levers C and E.

Assembling the Levers

1. Insert the crankshaft into the bearings box.

2. Fix the crank and pin F/G on to the end of the crankshaft.

3. Fit the lever support block A dowel pins into the side of the bearings box base.

4. Insert the short pivot block B dowel peg into the hole in the lever support block A.

5. Secure the slotted lever C by inserting a spindle J into the walls of the short pivot block B, so that the slotted lever C is held between them, moving freely on the pin.

6. Repeat Steps 3 and 4 for the tall pivot block D and plain lever E.

7. Fit the blocks H on to the ends of the levers C and E. Square pegs in round holes can make a good friction fit.

8. Operate the mechanism, either backwards or forwards, using the two types of lever.

 COLOUR AND NUMBER THE PARTS

THE BOX OF MECHANISMS

The mechanisms and their component parts are contained within this box. The importance of keeping them in order cannot be stressed too much, and colouring and numbering each part is the best way to do it.

Making the Box of Mechanisms

1. Use 8mm plywood for the box and 5mm plywood for the interior sections.

2. Cut the lid and base of the box, 372 × 343mm (14⅝ × 13½in).

3. Cut the front and back panels, 372 × 70mm (14⅝ × 2¾in).

4. Cut the side panels 327 × 70mm (12⅞ × 2¾in).

Each component should be keyed with the number of the section to which it belongs. Every dowel, collet and washer should be marked and coloured to the specifications on the 'automata mechanisms boxed' chart (see page 111).

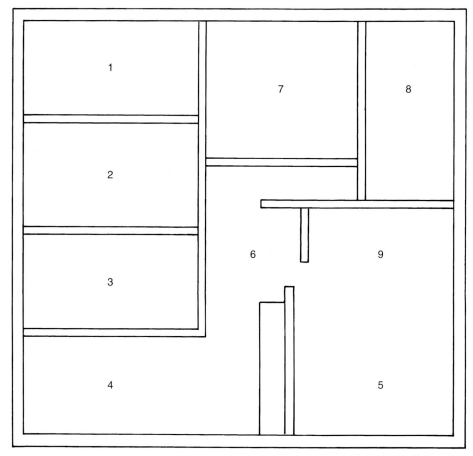

ONE-THIRD ACTUAL SIZE

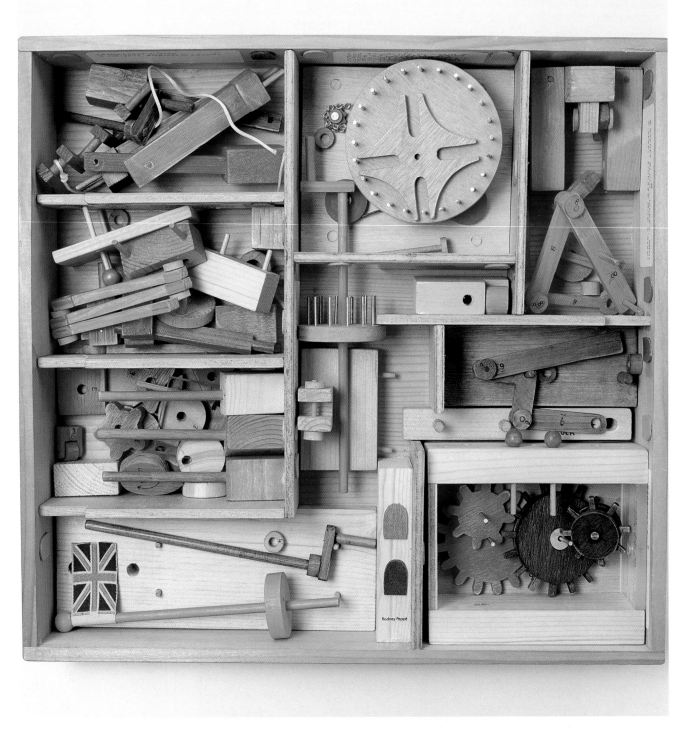

Each component has an allotted section in the box, which is to be found on the 'automata mechanisms boxed' chart (see opposite). In this way you can select whichever mechanism you wish and refer to the plan to which it belongs.

The Box of Mechanisms

Section	Automata Mechanisms Boxed	Plan	Colour
1	Double Crankshaft in 2 parts to fit into bearings box (Section 5). Dowel collet for end of shaft	5	Red
	The rest of the shaft and handle assembly	5	Blue
	Lever, block and pivot stand	6	Red
	Lever, block and pivot stand	6	Blue
2	4-bar linkage, comprising linkage bar, coupler and lever. Dowel collets and 2 spindles. Dowel collet for crank pin	8	Light brown
	Crank slider and 4-bar linkage peg board, with 2 fixed pins and two dowel pins with bead heads	4	Plain
	Crank pin, comprised of wheel and pin	All	Plain
	Bell crank and lever support block with 2 fixed pegs	9 and 15	Plain
	Crank slider, rod, circular bearing with peg, slotted bearings and 2 pegs. Block, washer and collet	4	Mauve
	Plain lever in pivot block	15	Brown
	Slotted lever in pivot block	15	Brown
3	5 cams for pin follower	2	Green
	5 cams for roller followers	2	Red
	Roller followers	3	Red
	Pin follower with block	3	Red
	Pin follower with block	3	Green
	2 pin followers with blocks	3	Plain
	2 disc followers	3	Plain
	Disc followers with restraining pin	3	Plain
	2 dowel pins with bead heads	3	Plain
	Perspex shield, or panel with fixed dowel pins	3	Plain
4	Plinth with location pegs for bearings box	8	Plain
	Crank handle and shaft with collet	1	Blue
	Friction-driven pole and driven disc	14	Yellow
5	Bearings box	1	Plain
	Backboard with pegs for bearings box	12	Plain
	Large and small cut gearwheels	12	Cerise
	Large and small strutted gearwheels	12	Dark blue
6	4-bar linkage pivot block and base with 2 dowel collets and spindle	8	Light Brown
	Small pin wheel shaft and handle	13	Light Yellow
	Friction-driven pole support block with 2 pegs and driver disc	14	Yellow
7	Bearings box backboard with pegs. Chain and sprocket wheels (from model shop). Drive band and pulleys	–	Plain
	Large pin wheel	13	Light Yellow
	Geneva wheel, comprised of large crank pin and shield, dowel spindle, collet and washer	11	Light Green
8	Ratchet assembly, comprised of 2 pillars with pegs, ratchet block and subsidiary panel with spring. Dowel shaft with 2 collets, driving pawl and 2 collets	10	Pink
	Linkage bar, lever, fixed bar with dowel pins, 2 dowel spindles and 4 collets. Collet for crank pin (crank pin itself is in Section 2)	–	Light brown
9	Bell crank, comprising lever, L-shaped arm with pivot pin and collet. Linkage bar with 2 spindles and 4 collets. Lever support block with peg. Dowel collet and washer	9	Blue
	Pin wheel bearing support arm with 2 pegs	13	Yellow

*Miniature automata mechanisms: seven of these little mechanisms use drawback springs to operate the machinery. The actual size can be seen on the cutting guide on the plan (*opposite*).*

5. Glue and pin the box together, leaving the lid till the end.
6. Cut the walls for sections 1, 2 and 3, 145 × 64mm (5¾ × 2½in).
7. Cut the long retaining wall for sections 1, 2 and 3, 254 × 64mm (10 × 2½in).
8. Glue the walls of these sections, as in the diagram, to the box. You will have spaces between the sections of 78mm (3 1/16in), 86mm (3⅜in) and 78mm (3 1/16in). This leaves a space for section 4 of 72mm (2 13/16in).
9. Cut a wall for section 5, 112 × 64mm (4⅜ × 2½in) and a support block from a batten 105 × 47mm (4⅛ × 1⅞in).
10. Cut a wall for section 9, 157 × 64mm (6 3/16 × 2½in) and a small section to support it, 47 × 64mm (1⅞ × 2½in).
11. Cut the wall between sections 6 and 7, 127 × 64mm (5 × 2½in). Cut out a rectangle, 44 × 51mm (1¾ × 2in), leaving 95mm (¾in) strip to glue to the long wall, supporting sections 1, 2 and 3.
12. Cut the last wall between sections 7 and 8, 143 × 64mm (5⅝ × 2½in).
13. Glue the remaining sections as on the diagram.
14. Attach the lid to the box, at the back, with a couple of brass hinges. (Butterfly hinges look nice.)
15. Fix two brass 'question-mark' latches to the edges of the lid at the front, with two little brass screws to hold them.
16. Finally, with the lid of the box securely fixed, the mechanisms should stay in their sections, even if the box is turned upside down.

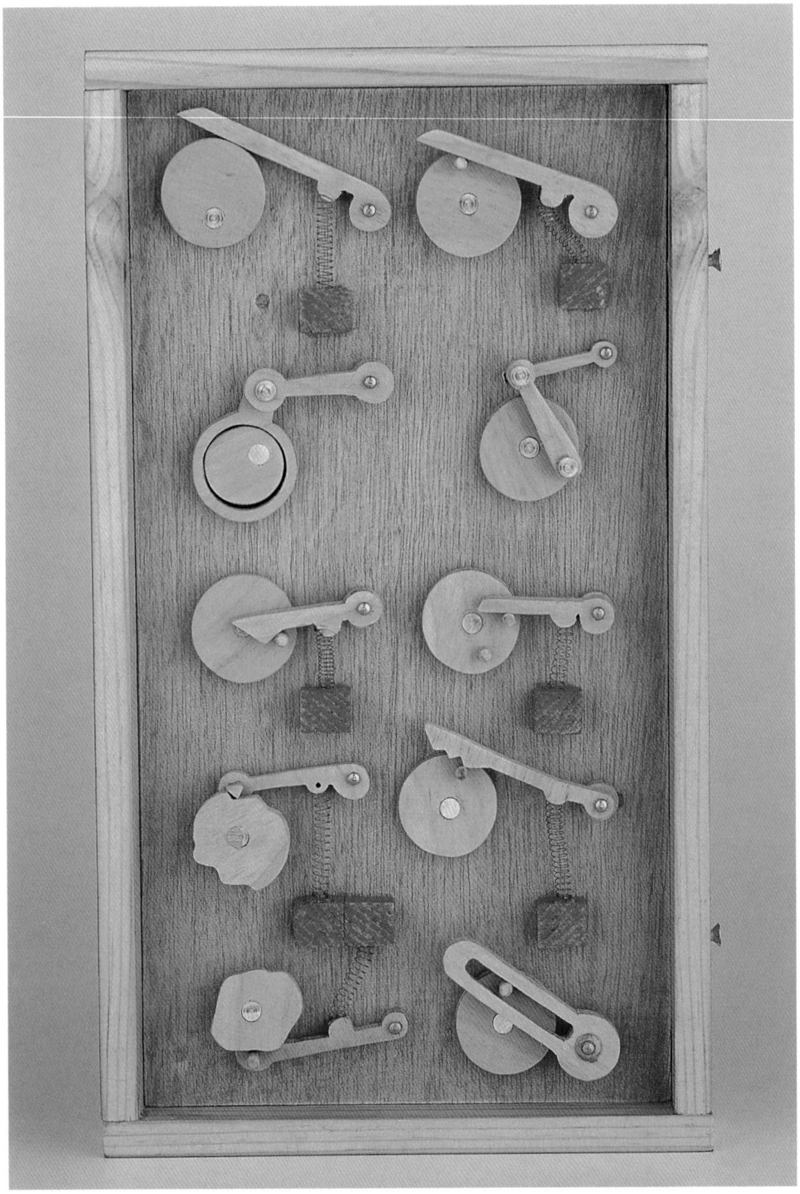

MAKING MINIATURE MECHANISMS

All the mechanisms are cut from 6mm plywood and should be positioned in the box as shown on the cutter guide (*see* page 113). The shafts are flat-headed and round-headed rivet pins, secured at the back with 10 × 3mm (⅜ × ⅛in) stripwood blocks. Beads, 10mm (⅜in) in diameter, attached to rivet shafts at the back, serve as easy-to-turn knobs when viewed from the front. (If flat-headed rivets are not available, use nails instead.)

Making the Box

The box can be constructed in the same way as the larger box. The difference is that the base, containing the mechanisms, must be positioned in the middle, to allow the box to

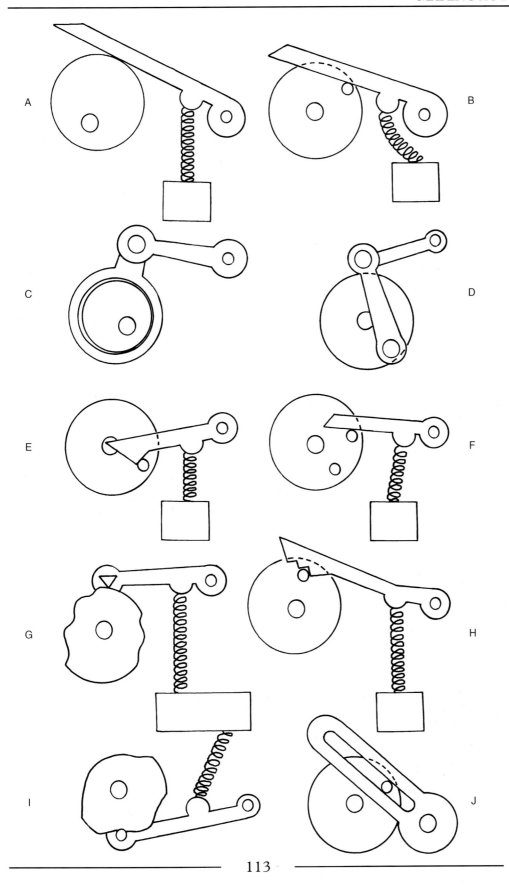

PLAN 16
**Miniature
Mechanisms**
*A: eccentric disc with
continuous movement;
B: eccentric crank pin with
continuous movement;
C: eccentric disc with
follower giving continuous
movement; D: eccentric
crank with connecting
rod, giving continuous
movement; E: eccentric
crank pin with slow and
sudden release of runner,
giving intermittent
movement; F: eccentric
double crank pin with
stepped and sudden
release of the runner,
giving intermittent
movement; G: cam and
runner with knife edge;
H: crank pin and shaped
runner giving a slow and
'nodding' release of the
runner; I: cam and runner
with pin; J: crank pin and
slotted runner.*

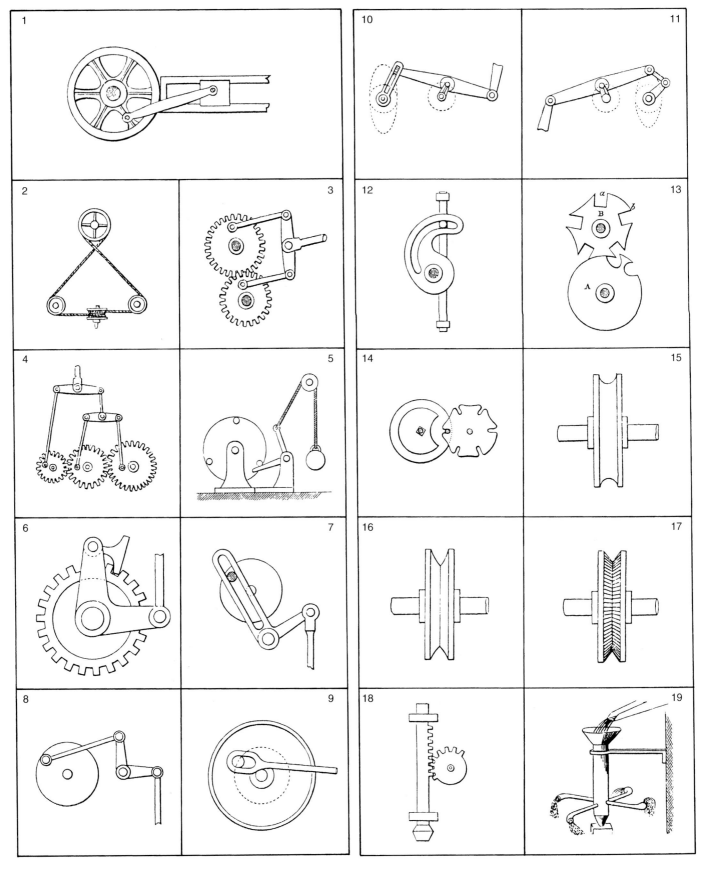

lie flat without touching the bead knobs. The lid must also be able to close without touching the mechanisms.

The dimensions of the box, made from 8mm (⁵⁄₁₆in) pine, are 254 × 146 × 47mm (10 × 5¾ × 1⅞in) with the lid closed. The plan shows the actual size of the inside area. Fix two brass latches and screws to the lid at the front, and brass hinges at the back, to secure the lid to the box. The back is left open for easy operation of the knobs.

ADDITIONAL MECHANISMS

The nineteen mechanisms listed opposite and below, which are especially useful to the automatist, are taken from Henry T. Brown's *Five Hundred and Seven Mechanical Movements* published in 1868.

1. Ordinary crank motion.
2. A method of transmitting motion from a shaft at right-angles to another whose axis is in the same plane.
3. The rotation of the two spur gears, with crank pins attached, produces a variable alternating traverse of the horizontal bar.
4. A more complex modification of No.3.
5. Circular motion into alternating rectilinear motion, by the action of the studs on the rotary disc upon one end of the bell crank, the other end of which has attached to it a weighted cord passing over the pulley.
6. Reciprocating rectilinear motion into intermittent circular motion by means of the pawl attached to the bell crank, and operating in the toothed wheel.
7. Circular motion into variable alternating rectilinear motion, by the crank pin on the rotating disc working in the slot of the bell crank.
8. A modification of No.7, a connecting rod being substituted for the slot in the bell crank.
9. The rotation of the disc carrying the crank pin gives a to-and-fro motion to

the connecting rod. The slot allows the rod to remain at rest at the termination of each stroke.

10. The slotted crank on the left is attached to the shaft, and the connecting rod that connects it with the reciprocating moving power has a pin that works in the slot of the crank. Between the first crank and the moving power is a shaft carrying a second crank, attached to the same connecting rod. While the first crank moves in a circular orbit, the pin at the end of the rod moves in an elliptical orbit, increasing the leverage of the main crank at those points most favourable for the transmission of power.
11. A modification of No.10, in which a link is used to attach the connecting rod to the main crank, dispensing with the slot shown in No.10.
12. By turning the shaft carrying the curved slotted arm, a rectilinear motion of variable velocity is given to the vertical bar.
13. The Geneva Stop, used in watches to limit the number of revolutions in winding up. The convex curved part a, b of the wheel B serves as the stop.
14. Another modification of the Geneva Stop.
15. A concave-grooved pulley for a round band.
16. A smooth-surfaced V-grooved pulley for a round band.
17. A V-grooved pulley with its groove notched to improve adhesion of the band.
18. Stamp. Vertical percussive falls derived from horizontal rotating shaft. The mutilated toothed pinion moves up the rack to raise the rod until its teeth leave the track and let the rod fall.
19. Barker's or reaction mill. Rotary motion of the central hollow shaft is obtained by the reaction of the water escaping at the ends of its arms. The rotation is in the reverse direction of the escape.

OPPOSITE PAGE:
Nineteen mechanisms especially useful to the automatist.

Conversion Table

Imperial and metric conversion table.
Comparative dimensions:
English–American (Imperial) and metric

Inches into millimetres

1/16in	=	1.6mm
1/8in	=	3.2mm
3/16in	=	4.7mm
1/4in	=	6.4mm
5/16in	=	7.9mm
3/8in	=	9.5mm
7/16in	=	11.1mm
1/2in	=	12.7mm
9/16in	=	14.3mm
5/8in	=	15.9mm
11/16in	=	17.5mm
3/4in	=	19.1mm
13/16in	=	20.6mm
7/8in	=	22.2mm
15/16in	=	23.8mm
1in	=	25mm
1¼in	=	32mm
1½in	=	38mm
1¾in	=	44mm
2in	=	51mm
2¼in	=	57mm
2½in	=	64mm
2¾in	=	70mm
3in	=	76mm
3¼in	=	82mm
3½in	=	89mm
3¾in	=	95mm
4in	=	102mm
4¼in	=	108mm
4½in	=	115mm
4¾in	=	121mm
5in	=	127mm
5¼in	=	133mm
5½in	=	140mm
5¾in	=	146mm
6in	=	152mm
6¼in	=	158mm
6½in	=	165mm
6¾in	=	171mm
7in	=	178mm
7¼in	=	184mm
7½in	=	191mm
7¾in	=	197mm
8in	=	203mm
8¼in	=	209mm
8½in	=	216mm
8¾in	=	222mm
9in	=	229mm
9¼in	=	235mm
9½in	=	242mm
9¾in	=	248mm
10in	=	254mm
10¼in	=	260mm
10½in	=	267mm
10¾in	=	273mm
11in	=	280mm
11¼in	=	285mm
11½in	=	292mm
11¾in	=	298mm
12in	=	305mm
13in	=	330mm
14in	=	356mm
15in	=	381mm
16in	=	407mm
17in	=	432mm
18in	=	457mm
19in	=	483mm
20in	=	508mm
21in	=	534mm
22in	=	559mm
23in	=	584mm
24in	=	610mm
25in	=	635mm
26in	=	661mm
27in	=	686mm
28in	=	711mm
29in	=	737mm
30in	=	762mm
40in	=	1,016mm
50in	=	1,270mm
60in	=	1,525mm
70in	=	1,779mm
80in	=	2,033mm
90in	=	2,287mm
100in	=	2,540mm

Feet into metres

1ft	=	0.3m
2ft	=	0.6m
3ft	=	0.9m
4ft	=	1.2m
5ft	=	1.5m
6ft	=	1.8m
7ft	=	2.1m
8ft	=	2.4m
9ft	=	2.7m
10ft	=	3.05m
20ft	=	6.1m
30ft	=	9.1m
40ft	=	12.2m
50ft	=	15.2m
60ft	=	18.1m
70ft	=	21.3m
80ft	=	24.4m
90ft	=	27.4m
100ft	=	30.5m
200ft	=	61m
300ft	=	91m
400ft	=	122m
500ft	=	152m
600ft	=	183m
700ft	=	213m
800ft	=	244m
900ft	=	274m
1,000ft	=	304.8m

Millimetres into Inches

1mm	=	0.04in
2mm	=	0.08in
3mm	=	0.12in
4mm	=	0.16
5mm	=	0.20in
6mm	=	0.24in
7mm	=	0.28in
8mm	=	0.32in
9mm	=	0.36in
10mm	=	0.4in
11mm	=	0.43in
12mm	=	0.47in
13mm	=	0.51in
14mm	=	0.55in
15mm	=	0.59in
16mm	=	0.63in
17mm	=	0.67in
18mm	=	0.71in
19mm	=	0.75in
20mm	=	0.79in
21mm	=	0.83in
22mm	=	0.87in
23mm	=	0.91in
24mm	=	0.95in
25mm	=	0.98in
26mm	=	1.02in
27mm	=	1.06in
28mm	=	1.10in
29mm	=	1.14in
30mm	=	1.18in
31mm	=	1.22in
32mm	=	1.26in
33mm	=	1.3in
34mm	=	1.34in
35mm	=	1.38in
36mm	=	1.42in
37mm	=	1.46in
38mm	=	1.5in
39mm	=	1.54in
40mm	=	1.58in
45mm	=	1.77in
50mm	=	1.97in
55mm	=	2.17in
60mm	=	2.36in
65mm	=	2.56in
70mm	=	2.76in
75mm	=	2.95in
80mm	=	3.15in
85mm	=	3.35in
90mm	=	3.54in
95mm	=	3.75in
100mm	=	3.94in
125mm	=	4.92in
150mm	=	5.9in
175mm	=	6.89in
200mm	=	7.87in
225mm	=	8.86in
250mm	=	9.84in
275mm	=	10.83in
300mm	=	11.81in
325mm	=	12.8in
350mm	=	13.78in
375mm	=	14.77in
400mm	=	15.75in
425mm	=	16.74in
450mm	=	17.72in
475mm	=	18.71in
500mm	=	19.69in
525mm	=	20.67in
550mm	=	21.65in
575mm	=	22.64in
600mm	=	23.62in
625mm	=	24.61in
650mm	=	25.59in
675mm	=	26.57in
700mm	=	27.56in
750mm	=	29.53in
800mm	=	31.5in
850mm	=	33.46in
900mm	=	35.43in
950mm	=	37.4in
1,000mm	=	39.4in

Metres into feet and inches

1m	=	3ft 3⅜in
2m	=	6ft 6¾in
3m	=	9ft 10in
4m	=	13ft 1½in
5m	=	16ft 5in
6m	=	19ft 8in
7m	=	22ft 11½in
8m	=	26ft 3in
9m	=	29ft 6½in
10m	=	32ft 10in
20m	=	65ft 7in
30m	=	98ft 5in
40m	=	131ft 3in
50m	=	164ft
60m	=	197ft
70m	-	230ft
80m	=	262ft
90m	=	295ft
100m	=	328ft
200m	=	656ft
300m	=	984ft
400m	=	1312ft
500m	=	1640ft
600m	=	1968ft
700m	=	2297ft
800m	=	2615ft
900m	=	2953ft
1,000m	=	3281ft

MAKERS' WORK

Rodney Peppé

I trained as an illustrator at the Central School of Art in London before spending five years in advertising. I went freelance in 1965 as a consultant graphic designer which gave me the opportunity to do my first children's book, published in 1968. Since then there have been over eighty titles and two television series.

My interest in automata and moving toys evolved from making wooden lay figures to draw my picture book characters. The first of these was 'Henry', a rather incompetent two-legged elephant. The interest turned to inspiration when I met Sam Smith. He was a beacon for many toymakers and automatists. He certainly lit my fire. The encouragement he engendered wasn't exactly offered; it was there in his work, by example, in this wonderfully generous and creative man.

I began to make highly decorated jumping jacks, which were seen by a publisher who wanted to do a book on making wooden toys. I was asked to do a chapter on fretwork and wound up doing the whole book, Moving Toys *(published in 1980), with complete plans for every toy.*

The combination of meeting Sam Smith and making all the toys for the book turned my creative life around. While wearing the hats of author, illustrator and graphic designer I now donned a toymaker's hat which eventually led to an automatist's hat. Sometimes I wear all the hats at once and feel like a character from Dr Seuss.

'The Twelve Days of Christmas' 1990
(838 × 432 × 57mm/33 × 17 × 2¼in)
An exploration of simple mechanisms, mostly cams. Everything moves, except the Five Gold Rings. The Nine Ladies Dancing only move their legs.

'Tyger! Tyger!' 1992
(432 × 419 × 229mm/17 × 16½ × 9in)
The two handles move the legs, open the jaw, change the eyes and operate three birds. One is hidden in the jungle, which is marbled MDF.

'Uncle Sam's Whirligig' 1985
(368 × 280 × 424mm/14½ × 11 × 9½in)
My homage to whirligigs in the State of Maine, USA. Strictly for show, not for blow.

'Jumping Jacks' 1978/1984
(356 × 127 × 57mm/14 × 5 × 2¼in)
I've been making these for years. They are painted wood and collage of printed ephemera.

'Musical Clown' 1978
(222 × 136 × 152mm/8¾ × 5⅜ × 6in)
I made this for my book *Moving Toys*. It is based on 'Le Clown Orchestre', from Victor Bonnet's 1925 catalogue of Martin toys. I used my own string mechanism.

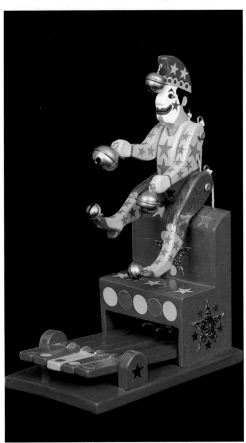

'Musical Clown', 1978.

'The Twelve Days of Christmas' by Rodney Peppé, 1990.

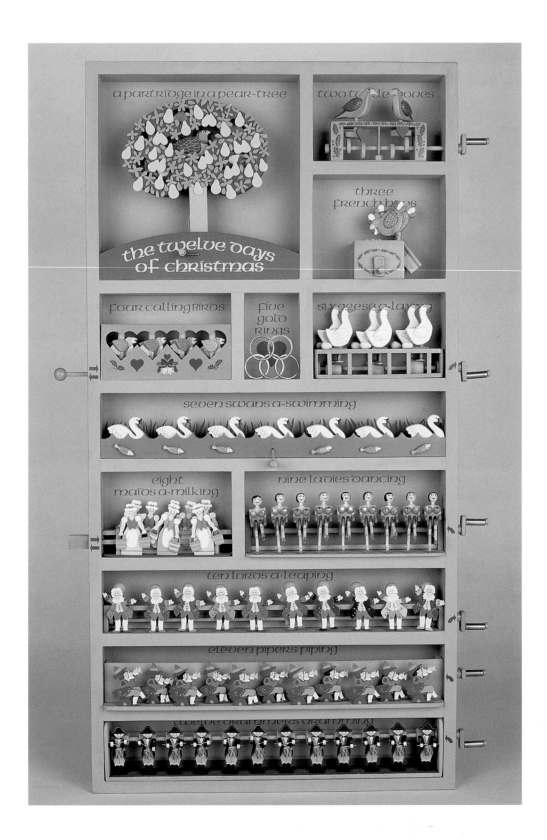

FAR LEFT: 'Tyger! Tyger!',
1992.

'Uncle Sam's Whirligig',
1985.

Jumping jacks,
1978/1984.

'Tender to Thalia' by Robert Race.

Robert Race

What I like most of all in making automata is trying to combine a striking image with a simple mechanism that really makes full use of the particular properties of the materials. It's pretty difficult to do. When you get it right, even quite rudimentary movements can give an irresistible illusion of animation. This works in spite of the mechanism being in full view; indeed, that seems to add to the magic.

If the principal movement is rather irregular, like that produced by a crank, it helps to have something dangling free, or wobbling on a wire, which will move less predictably. This should help to make the total movement more lively and more lifelike.

At best a simple image will expand into a story, or stories … people will often remember a successful piece as having a lot more complicated movements than it really has. Once the illusion of animation takes hold, the gaps get filled in, the stories grow.

I enjoy using driftwood a lot: partly because of the business trips to the seaside; partly because of the extraordinary range of wood that comes floating along the English Channel; and partly because of the depth of character it seems to acquire from the surface effects of sea creatures, saltwater, pounding waves and sunshine.

'Walkies'.

'Demented Ruminants'.

'Moon Priest'.

'Blackbird and Wasp'.

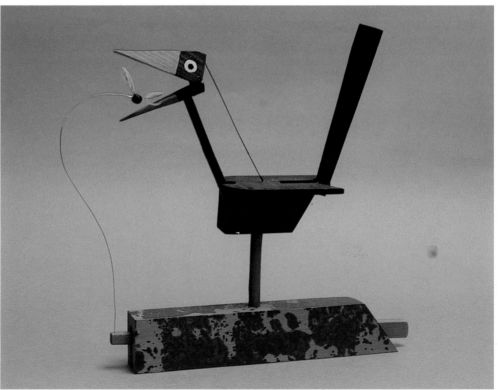

Martin Smith

The automata of artist and inventor Martin Smith have developed from a fascination for all things that move. He creates humorous macabre figures, which are beautifully crafted from wood and metal. The principal aim is to entertain and charm. Mechanisms are exposed in order to deny any secrecy; it is reassuring and immensely satisfying to observe the hypnotic motion of the cams and levers. Working from his studio in the north of England, Smith has been developing and producing his intriguing sculptures for several years. His work has been welcomed into art galleries, community spaces, corporate corridors and people's homes.

'The Cuckoo's Clock'

On the hour and for a small fee the four girls perform their act, the mating call of the cuckoo! Flapping arms, gaping mouths and undulating breasts, they do it all and in sequence. The figures are carved from limewood and the clock case is built using tinplate steel. The piece measures around 185cm high, 45cm wide and 45cm deep (73 × 18 × 18in).

Details of 'The Cuckoo's Clock' by Martin Smith.

*'The Cuckoo's Clock' by
Martin Smith.*

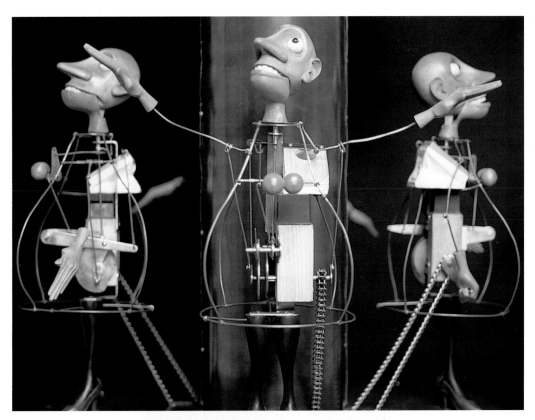

Details of 'The Cuckoo's Clock' by Martin Smith.

6 THEME PROJECTS

The two themes explored here are intended to serve as a springboard or starting point for your own invention. The first theme project is based on the 'Twelve Days of Christmas' and the second is a jumping jack. The projects are designed to be looked at in one way and seen in another. The difference between looking and seeing, here, is absorbing the reference and seeing what you can do with it. Slavish copying deprives the maker of the supreme experience of invention. If creativity is encouraged, originality will flourish and the end result will prove to be far more satisfying and rewarding.

Sometimes ideas are hard to come by:

> You beat your pate,
> And fancy wit will come:
> Knock as you please,
> There's nobody at home.
>
> (Alexander Pope)

Do not despair. There are many ideas in the public domain. For example, 'The Twelve Days of Christmas' is not an idea that belongs to any one person; it is more of an institution and therefore available to all. It began as a rhyme or chant, first appearing in a small children's book called *Mirth Without Mischief*, published in London in about 1780. It is therefore free of copyright, which runs out seventy years after an author's death (its author is unknown, anyway, and 'Anon' does not have many teeth in matters of copyright). The real 'idea' is born when a maker decides to take such an institution or concept and says what he or she has to say. Material from the public domain is free for all to use and it is that use that is crucial in determining the success of the finished piece. For example, when an illustrator makes a contribution to an author's book, the idea is supplied by the author, but the illustrator embellishes and even enhances the work.

Children's literature provides a rich source of characters and incidents, especially the old nursery rhymes, which are in the public domain, with more than a sprinkling of Anons. Adult literature, from Chaucer to Shakespeare and beyond, also offers a wide choice of themes. For example, 'Tyger! Tyger!' and 'A Different Drummer' (Rodney Peppé) are something of a homage to William Blake and Thoreau, both exponents in their own ways of individual intuition. Creativity can spring from a source without being indigenous to it and can, indeed, flourish within hybridization.

Literature in the public domain is not your only source of ideas, of course; ideas and themes are everywhere you look, as long as you are open to them. One productive time for the imagination is that no-man's-land between drowsiness and sleep, when the mind is relaxed and not trying to think of ideas. (A relaxed state often encourages the brain to give form to that terrific idea that may have been somewhere on the periphery for some time.) The zoo and the circus are strong subjects that have interested artists and automatists for years. There are some people who find zoos and circuses controversial, however, and they may prefer to find their inspiration in other subjects featuring animals, such as Noah's Ark.

Writing lists can often help to give form to ideas because each item can trigger an idea or succession of ideas into a theme. The acquisition of ideas is a personal thing and everyone has their own methods of working. One thing is certain, however: nobody can explain *exactly* how it is done. The idea may not be there one moment and, the very next moment, there it is!

'THE TWELVE DAYS OF CHRISTMAS' (RODNEY PEPPÉ)

Each section of the 'The Twelve Days of Christmas' (*see* photo on page 118) took about a week to make, fitted in around other work. The intention is not that you should endeavour to make this piece in its entirety, but that you should use it as inspiration.

A Partridge in a Pear Tree

The handle winds a string, which makes the partridge dip forward while foliage 'doors' snap shut, to give the effect that the bird has flown. Two identical trees were cut together to accommodate the bar upon which the partridge pivots. Pears and leaves were cut out, painted and stuck to the tree.

Two Turtle Doves

These two lovebirds turn to and from one another with a brief kiss (or is it a nod?), while their hearts shadow their actions. The camshaft is fixed with four eccentrically set cams, which, by friction, turn the discs attached to the doves. The central upright bar prevents the birds from spinning too far.

Three French Hens

The hens peck at (real) corn glued to the top surface of the box. They are programmed to peck in rotation by cams, which activate key-shaped counterweights. Their tail feathers proclaim their nationality, while a seasonal wreath encircles the handle.

Four Calling Birds

The birds swivel to face the front and back again in their heart-shaped windows. A lever pushes and pulls the feathered quartet,

who are fixed to rotating pillars attached to the lever by strings.

Five Gold Rings

These are not gold and remain obstinately static. Two small hole saws were used to cut out the skin (aero) ply rings 1.5mm ($\frac{1}{16}$in) thick. Interlocking is simply done by making a cut in each ring and obscuring the incision with another ring.

Six Geese A-Laying

Each pair rise and fall in sequence, activated by cams placed at different angles to the shaft. The eggs are modelled in white Milliput, a compound for mending china, so they did not need painting.

Seven Swans A-Swimming

The swans bob back and forth in the waves followed by the fish. The central handle,

'A Partridge in a Pear Tree' – finished coloured design for one part of 'The Twelve Days of Christmas' (Rodney Peppé), shown complete on page 118.

Nine Ladies Dancing

The 'Bluebelles' kick their legs in unison, activated by cams that use the troupe's derrières as followers. (I have also made a much larger version of this troupe, with one dancer who was out of step and blushing, while others turned their heads to stare.)

Ten Lords A-Leaping

The noble lords, jointed at the knees, jump and sway in a very celebratory mood. Pear-shaped cams operate each vertical pillar, weighted with a wooden bead, attached to every figure.

Eleven Pipers Piping

As they tap their feet, the musicians lean forward and backward, playing their pipes. They are jointed at the waist and are hand-cranked, anti-clockwise. One visiting collector turned the handle the wrong way and broke the mechanism. Fortunately, all the automata are removable for repairs. (Always leave a safety hatch.)

Twelve Drummers Drumming

The drummers strike four beats to the bar – little square cams on a long shaft. Twenty-four of them engage with small wire loops attached to each drummer's shoulders, setting up a rapid drumbeat. Sometimes very long camshafts need to be supported, as they may warp.

Design Considerations

The 'Twelve Days' characters are designed to have a certain homogeneity, playing against the backdrop of a rural environment. The Nine Ladies Dancing may seem urbane, but they could be performing in a tent at a country fair. The choice of backdrop is merely intuitive scene setting, but it is an important factor in making automata, for it can influence colour selection. 'The Twelve Days of Christmas' is painted all over in a soft grey-green, which, with the red lettering, has Christmas connotations.

TOP: 'Milkmaid', 'Piper' and 'Lord' – finished coloured design for 'The Twelve Days of Christmas' (Rodney Peppé), shown complete on page 118.

ABOVE: Template drawings by Rodney Peppé for 'The Twelve Days of Christmas' (see page 118).

made from sturdy piano wire, is linked to thinner piano wires extending in both directions to each swan and fish. Rivets are made with discs from a paper punch, and instant glue is applied to the wire ends. (This is the method of fixing throughout.)

Eight Maids A-Milking

Two mini-magnets on a horizontal shaft enable these country maidens to swing their hips and buckets. Each bucket is covered with painted tin veneer, which reacts to the moving magnetic shaft that slides through the party wall.

More importantly, it suggests a soft country look and sets off the bright colours of the characters.

The use of colour is of variable significance to automatists. Some use none at all. Some apply just a touch, as a foil to the wood or metal, while others use it as an integral part of their work. Essentially, colour can be seen as a decorative add-on factor in the making of automata; the real business is *movement*. That is not to say that colour is merely cosmetic, but makers need to use their intuition to decide whether what they have to say needs colour.

Whatever theme you choose, you will need to determine the shape and size of the construction to house the automata, and to ascertain where the operating handles will be positioned. Try to use as many different mechanisms as possible, incorporating push-pull levers as well as crank handles. You may not wish to contain your theme within a box frame, but extend it to several boxes, with lids, containing theme automata. The related boxes would have to stack pleasingly, without any unsightly projections. To adapt 'The Twelve Days of Christmas' to this format would necessitate halving and widening the four long sections, placing the figures in two rows, like the Eight Maids.

THE JUMPING JACK OR *PANTIN*

The second project is a simpler one: considering different ways of making and decorating a jumping jack. The toy itself has a very old and colourful history. A childish craze for jumping jacks swept through France in 1746, but the police banned these dancing *Pantins*, reasoning that women were in danger of bearing babies with twisted limbs! With the passage of time, and the jumping jacks' firmly established place in the nursery, it might be safe to embark on making one.

Jumping jack (Rodney Peppé) made from painted wood and a collage of printed ephemera.

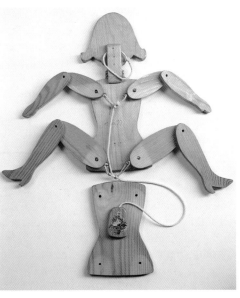

Reverse of the jumping jack, showing stringing.

See the photos above for the decorated jumping jack; in the lower photo, the reverse is shown with the back removed, to show the stringing. It can be seen that the limbs are formed in two parts, to allow ample movement.

To make a jumping jack you will need the following:

◆ some ⅜in (9.5mm)-thick wood (use deal if you want a grain, and ply if you do not);

- four countersunk No.8 screws, 1¼in (32mm) long;
- four countersunk No.8 screws, ⅞in (22mm) long;
- some thin string for connecting the limbs;
- thicker string for the toggle;
- glue (gum arabic or watered-down PVA); and
- four small screw eyes for the limbs.

Cutting and Drilling

The head and body are cut out of softwood (deal) or plywood ⅜in (9.5mm) thick, in one piece. The back and the limbs are cut out separately, the latter in pairs (temporarily bonded together), if your saw will allow.

Four holes are drilled in the body, wide enough to take No.8 screws loosely. Likewise, two holes are drilled, top and bottom in the upper part of the arms and legs. Small pilot holes are drilled, for No.8 screws, in the lower arms and legs and four pilot holes in the back. Countersink the holes in the body and the holes in the lower part of the upper arms and legs to take the heads of No.8 countersunk screws.

Cut out a hanging block to suspend the jumping jack and a toggle for the pull string. Drill a hole in the side, 9.5mm (⅜in) from the top of the hanging block, to take a thin string. Drill a hole vertically through the toggle to take a thicker pull string and widen the hole at the base to accommodate a triple knot.

Decorating

Paint, apply collage to, or decorate by any means all parts of the jumping jack, except the back and reverse of the limbs. Any printed ephemera can be pasted on with liquid glue (watered-down PVA) or gum arabic. This can be applied to both sides of the paper as it will stretch out, but do allow a minute before applying.

Once the paper or pieces of paper are positioned, if you are making a collage, cut tabs around the edges and fold them round so that they stick to the reverse.

Burnish these down, and allow the pieces to dry on the blocks so that they do not stick to the surface. They can be sprayed or painted with lacquer when dry.

The reverse sides, which will face the wall, can now be trimmed and sanded off. The reverse of the body does not need to be sanded as it will be covered by the back, which is undecorated. Pierce all the holes so that they are clear to receive screws.

Assembly

First, insert the four long screws through the front of the body and the top part of the upper limbs. Next. insert the four short screws through the lower part of the upper limbs and screw into the pilot holes in the lower limbs. Thread thin string through the screw eyes of the arms and secure with a knot. Do the same for the legs (*see* the photo opposite).

A central, thicker pull string is tied and knotted at the middle of the string between the arms. Likewise, the pull string is tied and knotted on the lower string. Trial and error will determine the amount of slack to leave when the figure is hanging on the wall. When you are satisfied that the arms and legs all work correctly, screw into the back, but not so tightly that it prevents freedom of movement.

The hanging block is now glued and pinned at the back of the neck and a thin string inserted as a knotted loop. The toggle receives the pull string through the top hole, which is then triple-knotted and accommodated in the recess at the base of the toggle.

Finishing

Using Milliput or similar modelling compound, roll it into little balls and flatten them on the eight visible screw heads. Allow time for them to dry out before painting. Remember, the more different you can make your jumping jack from other people's, the happier you should be!

MAKERS' WORK

Paul Spooner

I first made mechanical pieces when I was at college – a machine that wrote 'picasso' on a visiting card, a fruit machine that combined words instead of pictures to produce art critical phrases and a machine that moved so slowly you had to photograph it at hourly intervals to know it was moving, and a yawning machine that I could stand in front of other people's paintings. All of these things were made in the context of art school. When I left, the context changed and, for a time, the work stopped. This was in 1969.

My reasons for taking up automata making were rooted in those interests at college, which I think derive partly from a nerdish concern with machines for their own sake but also from the wish to convey meaning – the mechanism being the medium through which a story or joke is told, adding action to plot and character.

I suspect that there are parallels between the plot of a story or a joke and a mechanical device: like a spring mechanism that is loaded then released, the build-up and the punch line. Other machines mimic the shaggy-dog story, always returning to its starting point, recycling as long as the handle is turned. Then there is the option available both to toymakers and story-tellers; that of combining odd elements to produce absurd effects.

I've tried to add resonance to my work by including slightly macabre or erotic elements. The figure of Anubis appears from time to time, often involving himself in activities that would mortify the Ancient Egyptians for whom he was an important deity, with a crucial role in their death rituals. I often prefer his jet black, sometimes grotesquely attenuated head and slitty eyes to ordinary human features. When I make people's heads they usually convey innocence, bewilderment and not a little stupidity, so Anubis lends an air of seriousness and malevolence to the proceedings which, given the right context – a keep-fit session for example – increases the absurdity.

My first Anubis and I think the first piece I made for Cabaret Mechanical Theatre (1979) presented him sitting at a table drawing – or seeming to draw – a sausage. This was a good combination of mechanism and story in that I discovered a linkage that translated a rotary motion in the crank handle into a sausage-shaped movement of a pointer on to which I fixed Anubis' hand holding a pencil. The sausage was appropriate because Anubis, as Lord of the Mummy Wrappings, was associated with the parcelling up and preservation of the recently dead. It might have been this fortunate simultaneous discovery of mechanism and meaning that has made me continue featuring Anubis in the hope that such a happy accident might recur.

There are times when I borrow from art history to give extra meaning to my work. My version of Manet's 'Olympia' incorporates several features of the original – the nude, who writhes on the couch, and the cat, whose movements echo hers, plus a visiting Anubis who, as the caption tells, is doing a favour for the pharaoh in supplying Camp Coffee to Olympia in an attempt to keep her awake all weekend.

'*A Quiet Day at the Arm and Leg Shop*' 1992
The shop assistant looks around for potential customers.

'*The Mill Girl and the Toff*' 1987
The toff kneels and presents a ring to the ordinary girl, whose eyes pop out. A mahogany coffin with a coronet and a rough pine coffin stencilled 'Nobody' spin below.

'*Manet's Olympia*' 1981
With Anubis in attendance.

'*Nelson Mandela and Terry Waite go Shopping*' 1992
A little spring-mounted piece using alarm clock balance springs.

'*San Francisco and the San Andreas Fault*' 1993
Another clock spring mobile.

'A Quiet Day at the Arm
and Leg Shop' by Paul
Spooner, 1992.

'The Mill Girl and the Toff', 1987.

'Nelson Mandela and Terry Waite Go Shopping', 1992.

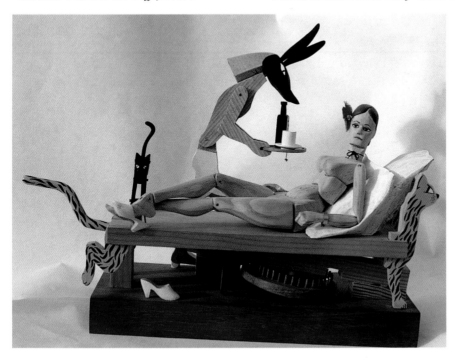

'Manet's Olympia', 1981.

'San Francisco and the San Andreas Fault', 1993.

'Meg and her Magic Lantern' by Melanie Tomlinson, 1997.

Melanie Tomlinson

My bicycle automata are inspired by the Eastern European circus and decorative arts. I am particularly interested in Eastern European children's literature and the wonderful, vibrant paintings found in Orthodox churches. Each piece I create consists of a figure attached to a unicycle, penny farthing or regular bicycle, operated by turning a handle. The mechanism (one or two cams and a rubber band) is simple, yet very effective, causing the figures to rock precariously from side to side, whilst pedalling furiously.

Although clients sometimes give me a specific brief when commissioning automata, the colours and shapes of the circus always find their way into my work. 'Lady Char' was commissioned by a collector of bicycles and teapots in New York. The buyer of 'Meg and Her Magic Lantern' was a Victorian magic lantern enthusiast and this piece lights up, casting a kaleidoscope of colourful patterns against the walls of a dark interior. 'Becky's Birds' and 'Dottie and Doris's Day Out' were based on two ladies I knew, who looked after birds.

Having originally trained in 3-D illustration, I pay particular attention to detail and each piece of metal I use is carefully selected. I create my pieces from a combination of copper, anodized aluminium and tin that I print myself. I also use a small amount of recycled tin, which often incorporates typography and is a mysterious addition to my work for its unknown origins.

My automata always sit on top of a box that can be opened and used as a container, but also to hide or lock away secret things!

'Lady Char', 1997.

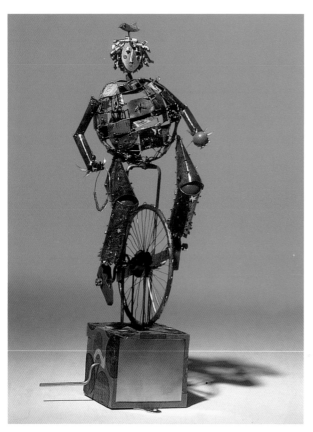

ABOVE: *'Becky's Birds',*
1998.

ABOVE RIGHT: *'Dottie and*
Doris's Day Out', 1998.

'Whiskers and Kittens',
1998.

Douglas Wilson

I am inspired by making something surprising out of virtually nothing. Using only plier snips and wire, I twist and turn caricatures of scenes and animals out of 20 different kinds of wire. I like wire, as it is very forgiving to people who are bad at drawing and can be very useful for encouraging artistic confidence in children and 33-year-old Scottish automatists.

When I started in 1996, I had no idea what 'automata' meant – and still am not sure – but could not have chosen a better craft field to work in. It combines my product design and graphics background with a childish line in cartoons, animals and toys. My initial inspiration came from an Alexander Calder exhibition of his wire circus, and the wire toys made by kids in many African countries.

Making mechanisms out of wire can be limiting and I am introducing more complex cams, gears, and so on, along with complementary materials to produce many more humorous, quirky and elegant wire automata.

BELOW LEFT: 'Horse', 2001.

BELOW: 'Belly Dancer', 2001.

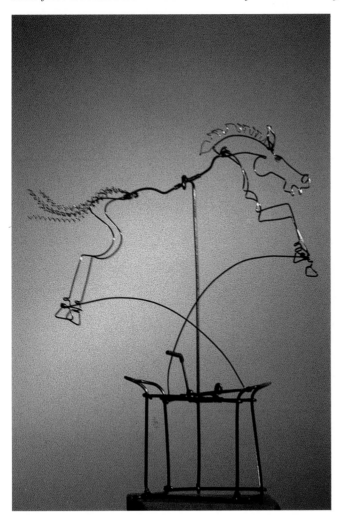

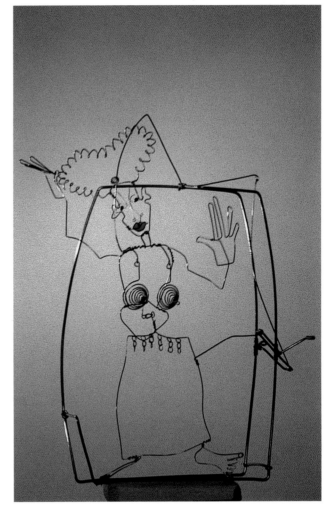

*'Woman Diver' by
Douglas Wilson, 2001.*

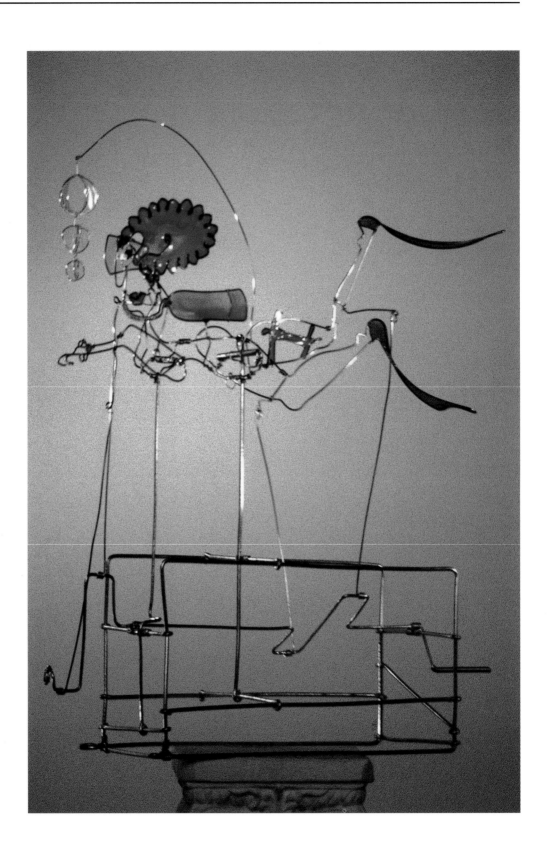

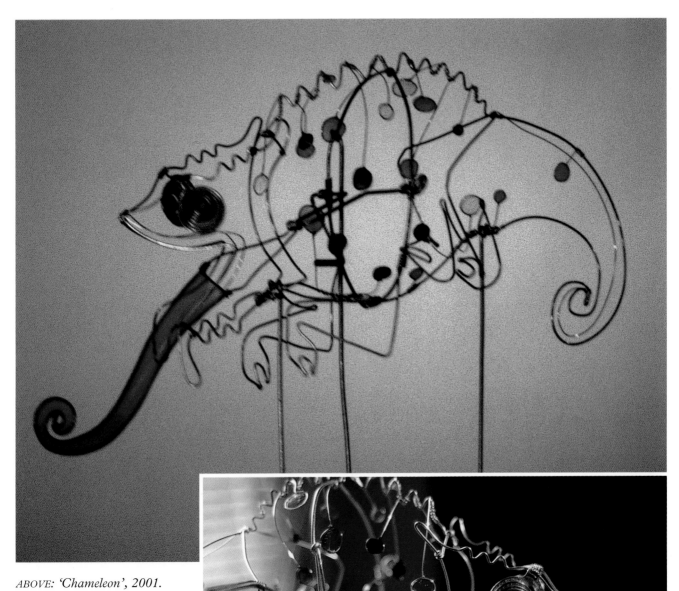

ABOVE: 'Chameleon', 2001.

RIGHT: Detail of 'Chameleon'.

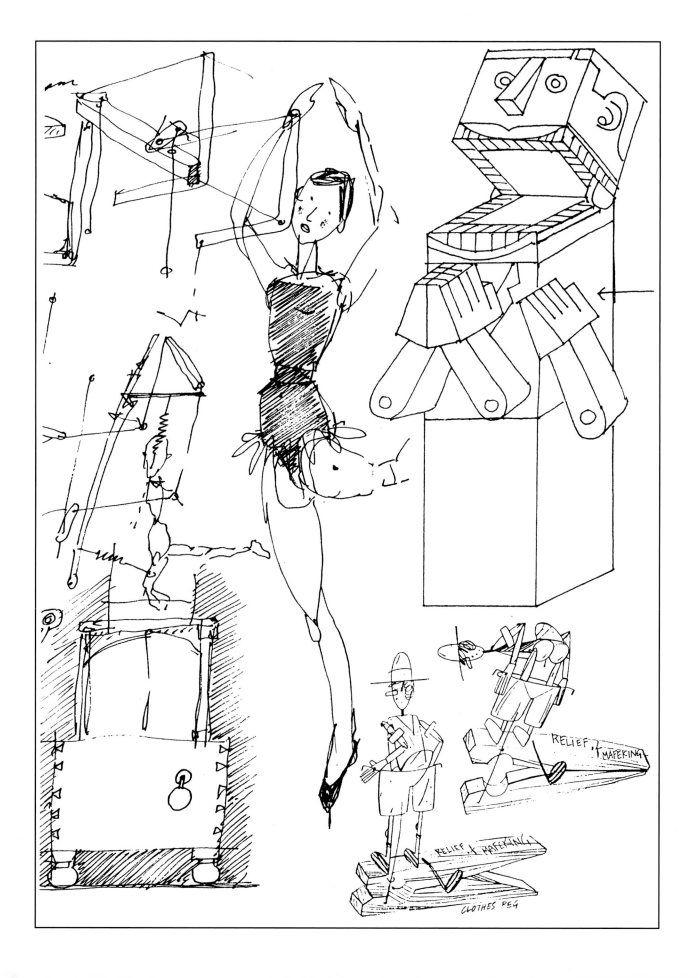

RELIEF MAFEKING

RELIEF MAFEKING

CLOTHES PEG

7 DESIGN

Note: this chapter is aimed primarily at the beginner. It incorporates the designs of Paul Spooner, Peter Markey and Ron Fuller.

PLANNING, DRAWINGS AND MODELS

'Design' is the matrix upon which all successful projects are based. Without it there would be no direction, and schemes would explode like malfunctioning rockets. Design involves not only planning in advance how a piece will work and look, but is also an integral part of every mechanical and artistic decision. This is not a question of high-tech ergonomics, but good design dictates whether the project is actually going to work and fulfil its aesthetic potential.

Design is the delineation on paper of a particular intention, or the making of a sketch model. The process is encapsulated in the Swiss painter and graphic artist Paul Klee's reference to the concise remark of a child, explaining how he draws: 'I think and then I draw a line round my think.' Design does not have to be an accurate blueprint; some of the best designs have been scribbled on the back of an envelope. Some makers do not much like doing roughs because they think better in a three-dimensional way. Some are happier handling mechanisms and testing their performances physically, rather than having to convert a 3-D idea into 2-D drawings. Individuals should work in the way that suits them best, but it is worth remembering that making preliminary sketches or models provides protection against disaster.

The case for not doing roughs, especially for the beginner, is a flimsy one, but it is true that disaster can sometimes be turned to the maker's advantage. Navigating uncharted waters can be exciting and rewarding. Hazards test problem-solving skills, and may even lead to inspiration and the perfect solution.

The enemy of design is the glitch, a gremlin waiting to strike just when you think everything is working wonderfully. To provide maximum protection against glitches, make a prototype model out of card. This is a quick and cheap method of identifying in advance any pitfalls and snags. The advantage of a model over a drawing is that any mistake in construction will be obvious, because the model will fail to work. Using glue, tape and scissors you can physically adapt or change the design of your model before it is too late. This is a much surer method than simply hoping the design will be all right. Once the prototype has been made, and all the adjustments completed, you will be confident at least that the mechanisms will work, and you will know what the piece will look like.

COMMISSIONS

Some automatists make preliminary drawings before building prototypes, but many have their own mentally built-in cams and cogs, which operate their individual methods of working. No two are the same. If you are engaged on a commission, however, drawings may be required by the client, unless some other means of presentation can be sought. One way of generating discussion is to show previous work and use it as a reference.

Where more than one person is involved in commissioning, discussions may be more complex. Committees tend to take

OPPOSITE PAGE: Designs by Paul Spooner, Peter Markey and Ron Fuller.

the view that ten different opinions are better than one; remember, 'a camel is a horse designed by a committee'. It is doubtful if any creative work ever comes out of committees, so prevent your horse turning into a camel, as tactfully as you can.

Be wary of playing 'The Artist' if you are being commissioned by people whose major consideration is business. You should be able to justify your project on their terms, not your own. *You* are the outsider. Do not attempt to puzzle them or blind them with your art, but heed instead the words of Ogden Nash:

One rule of thumb:
too clever is dumb.

It is also known as the KISS – Keep It Simple, Stupid! – principle. In your eagerness to express yourself, it can be tempting to go overboard, but the essence of design is to learn to reject inessentials. Leanness of thought should be fundamental in shaping your ideas and you should jettison all the accumulated debris of the process of creation.

THE STYLE OF THE MAKER

The way a maker chooses and discards elements in designing a piece, the colours and tones he or she uses, are as individual and identifiable as his or her handwriting. It is

Sketchbook designs by Paul Spooner (see photos on pages 132–3).

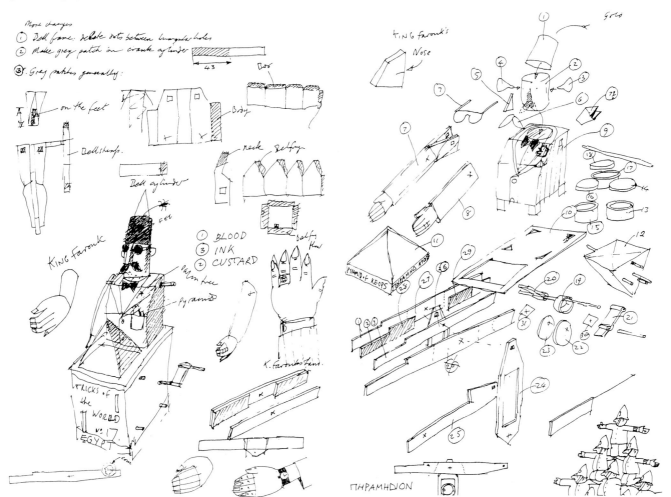

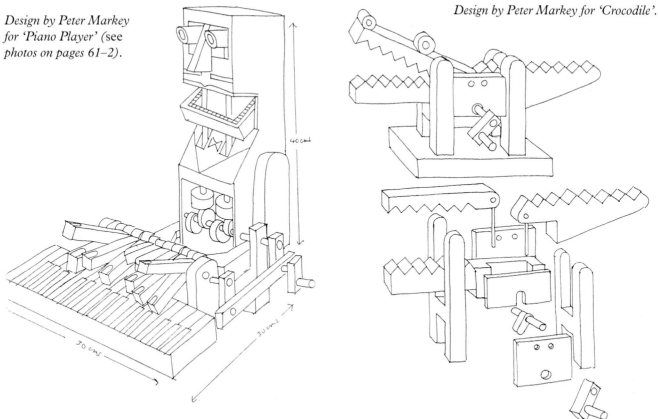

Design by Peter Markey for 'Piano Player' (see photos on pages 61–2).

Design by Peter Markey for 'Crocodile'.

that element known as 'style', the factor that defines the work of a particular maker.

This kind of style is clearly evident in the work of leading automatists Paul Spooner, Peter Markey and Ron Fuller. Apart from their shared influences and their connection with Susan Jackson's Cabaret Mechanical Theatre, these automatists in no way form a group. While they have spawned imitators, their individuality easily slips the knot of adulation, because their distinctive styles are strong enough to do so. A close look at their graphic work emphasizes how design shapes their output.

Paul Spooner shows in his sketchbook pages a mechanical and artistic mind spewing forth ideas as fast as he can get them down. The rapidity of thought is breathtaking. These are preliminary drawings for projects exploring and splicing together movement and artistry, which are inseparable, and conceived concurrently.

Lesser lights might envision sculptural forms and then animate them with mechanisms – it is a perfectly acceptable procedure, but it does not demand quite the same level of virtuosity.

Spooner is famous for his wry comments on contemporary life, often featuring Anubis, the Egyptian god of the dead (*see also* page 133).

Peter Markey is an advocate of the KISS principle. His work is distinctive for its simplicity and was greatly admired by the late Sam Smith. Using mainly geometric shapes, he achieves the most ingenious mobile effects, such as those enjoyed on his renowned 'wave machines'. Markey makes preliminary sketches followed by approximate-scale working drawings. Sometimes, when working on a commission, he will produce full-scale drawings. He favours exciting open mechanisms that add to the visual excitement of his automata.

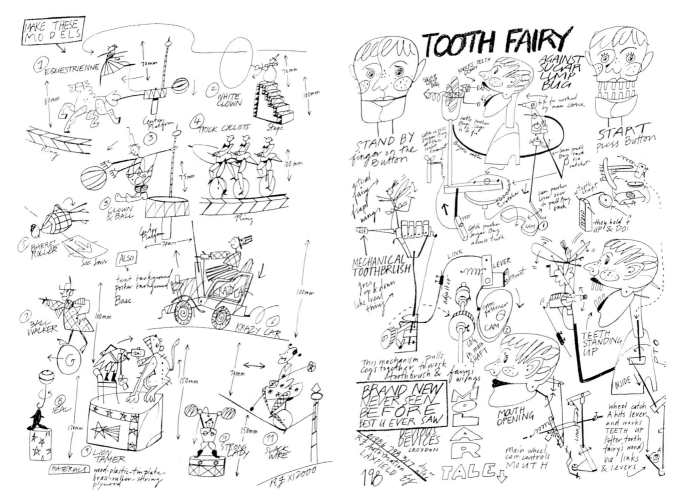

ABOVE: Design by Ron Fuller for 'Circus' (see photos on pages 23–4).

ABOVE RIGHT: Design by Ron Fuller for 'Tooth Fairy'.

Ron Fuller's stylish drawings are graphic fanfares for his pieces. Accompanied by amusing running commentaries, explaining how things work and what they do, they are printed on colourful A4 fliers. Fuller's approach is based firmly on the traditions of toymaking and folk art, which accounts for the bright colours of his pieces, which are often updates of traditional ideas. His 'Circus' is one of the humorous masterpieces of contemporary automata.

These three artists share a highly formal sense of visual and mechanical design, which directs their work. Each has his own particular hallmark, which identifies his pieces instantly; beyond that, they possess an individual approach to making automata, which comprises a blend of humour and irony. (It is an approach that seems to characterize the automata scene in Britain generally.) The homogeneity probably springs from their pioneering days in Falmouth, where Cabaret Mechanical Theatre was born.

Where do *you* start? At the beginning, of course. Start by designing something simple. Observe activities that are going on all around you: moving arms and legs, opening and closing mouths, and so on. Try to discover if observed actions can be translated into mechanical movements. Should you use a cam or a lever to operate the action? Do you need a linkage?

Above all, remember that, in design, less is more.

MAKERS' WORK

Kristy Wyatt Smith

I was brought up in a building that was both a home and a fine art/craft gallery. I also have a degree in illustration. This is the background to my work, and explains a lot of the elements within it: a drawn style, figurative qualities, working with or from a text, and an eclectic love of different materials and forms.

I find inspiration in a more decorative past. My subject matter is often imaginary idylls and stylized animals, which are more about representation than observation from nature. My use of reclaimed materials is an important factor in the aesthetics of the pieces. I enjoy the contradictory qualities of the rough surfaces and the unexpected delicate shapes of skip-found timber, strong colours of printed tin juxtaposed against age-battered wood.

The design process for me is a combination of written ideas, sketches and 3-D play. I follow intuition rather than a predesigned plan, and produce one-off pieces, or sometimes a small series of objects. I like to animate the figurative elements, however simply. The moving parts in the work are often referred to as automata. They are really too simplistic to earn that name and are just an element within the pieces rather than the whole point. The act of turning a handle engages the viewer, and hopefully captures them in the atmosphere of the piece.

My work is light and humorous, I hope that the pieces communicate a feeling, and a reaction. For me this is enough to justify their existence.

'Angel Convoy Over Breezy Tree Cupboard', 1998 (500 × 700 × 160mm/20 × 28 × 6¼in).

*'Blue Dog Cabinet' by
Kristy Wyatt Smith, 1999
(182 × 75 × 34cm/72 ×
29½ × 13in).*

*OPPOSITE PAGE:
(Top) 'Reclining Bather',
1999 (190 × 410mm/7½ ×
16in).*

*(Bottom left) 'I fear of
the Thunderbolt', 1998
(550 × 420 × 150mm/22 ×
16½ × 6in).*

*(Bottom right) 'Heat
Cupboard with Leaf
Tree Fans', 1999
(580 × 340 × 190mm/23 ×
13½ × 7½in).*

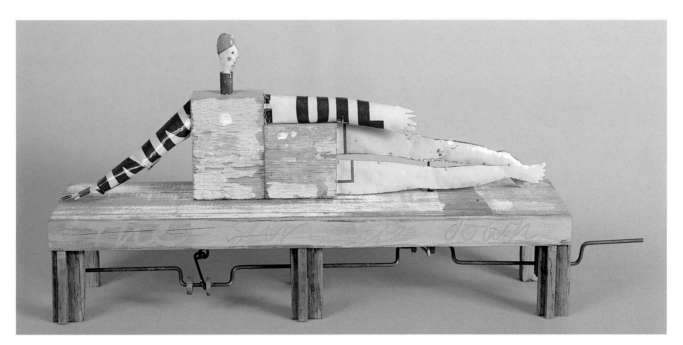

Vicki Wood

Over the last few years I have changed from making highly decorated work to using more recycled timber and bits and pieces. This can sometimes lead to problems on the mechanical side, but I think adds a further dimension of interest and fun to the work.

I particularly enjoy working on 'boxes' at the moment – there is an added feeling of secrecy as well as surprise.

'Sailor's Dream Chest' 1998

This is a cupboard to fix to the wall. Open the door and a startled mermaid pulls herself up behind a driftwood fish. The confused sailor wonders how he can reach her.

'Camelot' 1999

This piece uses ply and timber saved from an old watermill in Devon. It is operated by depressing the lever on the right of the box. King Arthur and Sir Lancelot have trouble controlling their mounts and Guinevere lifts her arms in despair. The portcullis lifts and the guard raises his sword.

'Trojan Horse'

Using old floorboards, rope and some 6mm ply, the operation is a simple opening of the door: the three Trojan warriors inside lift their spears as the guard outside looks over the door.

'The Sailor's Dream Chest' by Vicki Wood, 1998 (432 × 229 × 203mm/17 × 9 × 8in) (This page) Before operating. (Opposite page) After operating.

PAGE 150:
TOP: *'Trojan Horse' (356 × 305 × 152mm/ 14 × 12 × 6in). (Left) Before operating. (Right) After operating.*

BOTTOM: *'Camelot', 1999 (610 × 711 × 280mm/24 × 28 × 11in). (Left) Before operating. (Right) After operating.*

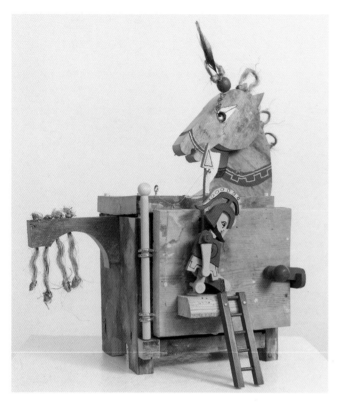

Jan Zalud

I was trained as a painter and began to work with wood in the late 1970s. My early puppets were strongly influenced by the traditional marionettes of Czechoslovakia where I was born and spent my early childhood. The first pieces were crudely carved from any timber I could find, and were simple both in feeling and mechanically.

Later the work developed into more refined automata. The wood used was predominantly lime, finely sanded and varnished. The images became more sophisticated, using heads or bodies to reflect various human conditions. Interaction with animals and with each other also became an occasional feature.

Although humour and wit are important facets of the work, I am aware of a sense of melancholy and possibly a hint of East European cynicism.

The mechanisms, sometimes simple and sometimes not, are generally open to viewing, either at the back or underneath, as part of the whole piece.

Coin-operated mechanism by Jan Zalud, at the Southampton City Art Gallery, 1986.

'Pretending to be a Fish and Paying the Price for It' by Jan Zalud, 1991.

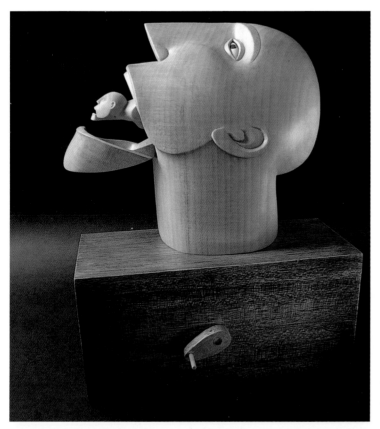

ABOVE LEFT: 'The Voice', 1991.

ABOVE: 'Fish Eating Birds', 1993.

'Hitchhikers', 1994.

8 PAINTING AND FINISHING

The method you use for painting and finishing really depends on the effect you are trying to achieve. Some automatists and toymakers do not paint their finished pieces at all, preferring to let the wood speak for itself.

PAINTING METAL AND WOOD

If you decide to paint metal, it generally requires a primer, whereas wood can be directly painted. The late, great Sam Smith used white emulsion as a primer to give brilliance to the Plaka colours he used, and many makers follow this procedure. If your piece incorporates much of the natural wood, with some painting, then it is easier, perhaps, to leave off the primer and paint extra coats as necessary. The finish applied to a piece is often the trademark of the maker – that unique quality that sets him or her apart from other makers, or his or her *style*.

There are no rules, but one tip worth noting is not to apply paint too thickly to a piece. Impasto looks great on a painting by Rouault or Van Gogh but it is quite unsightly, not to say impractical, on a piece with moving parts. The number of coats used is a matter of taste but two or three coats that will not chip or crack are probably a wise option.

Preparation

Sealers are available for sanding and knotting in timber (knots should be avoided where possible, anyway). B-I-N Primer Sealer is a quick-drying white pigment shellac, which sticks even to glossy surfaces. It is both a primer and undercoat.

A polyurethane lacquer spray, applied very briefly over the wood, will seal it for painting wet. If it is sprayed too heavily, the wet paint will be rejected. If that happens, wipe it off and rub spit on the surface to key it.

Primer is the first coat of paint on new work and should not be confused with an undercoat, which helps to cover previous coats of old paint. The primer seals the surface and is especially useful in preventing oil-based paints from sinking into it. White household emulsion paint is a serviceable primer, giving a lustrous base to enhance colours. Once applied, the primer should be lightly sanded with a fine abrasive to get rid of the high spots – those little fibres that pop up at the first sign of moisture.

Gesso fills in blemishes in the wood and should be sanded to an even finish before painting. Daler Rowney sell an acrylic gesso primer that is suitable for painting with acrylic or oils. It will take Plaka colour too, but it is quite expensive. Alternatively, though he seldom used it, try Sam Smith's own recipe for gesso:

> Equal quantities of whiting and water. Do not stir. Leave to stand for 15min. Pour off excess water. Add half quantity of glue – any liquid type but white synthetic best. Add a few drops of linseed oil. Stir mixture. It should be like thick cream. Add whiting if too thin, water if too thick.

Applying Colour

Staining can be done with either water- or spirit-based pigments. Coloured inks used with water can be flooded directly on to the wood, which must itself be wet. Since they are embedded in the wood, colour stains can never chip or flake off like paint. (For this reason, stains were used to colour the wooden mechanisms that illustrate automata movements in this book.)

Liberon produces a good range of spirit wood dyes, but Plaka colour or acrylic paints and inks, when watered down, can be used equally well for staining. They need less protection than do solid paints and they can be left unlacquered, if you feel that by lacquering you will lose, aesthetically, the subdued effect offered by staining. Lacquering darkens colours, especially on plywood, which has a grain that you may not wish to enhance. Always do a test before applying lacquer or varnish (see page 156).

Paint can be applied directly to the wood or over a white emulsion or gesso base. If painting wet on wood, unsightly spreading may occur. A brief light spray of lacquer will prevent this but too heavy a coat will result in rejection. There are many brands of paint available; Sam Smith used Plaka colour, an opaque casein emulsion that is lightfast and waterproof when dry. It needs lacquering or varnishing to protect its velvety-matt surface. Some acrylic paints have a wider colour range but are not all as opaque as Plaka. They do, however, have a pleasant sheen and some do not need an application of lacquer or varnish. These 'craft colours' come in plastic bottles with white flip-top lids.

Car sprays are excellent for covering large areas and for masking. They are glossy, quick-drying and sold in a vast range of colours in motoring shops. A matt spray can be used if a gloss effect is not required. There are a few precautions to follow for your own safety and that of others.

◆ Always wear a face mask, which you can buy from a chemists.
◆ Spray in a well-ventilated room or, if it is a still day, spray out of doors. Spraying in the wind is not recommended!

◆ The 'fall-out' of the spray is considerable and you will find a thin layer of coloured dust over everything if you are spraying for any length of time. Put down plenty of newspaper or, better still, sheets of plastic, which won't adhere so readily to the work.

The can should be at room temperature and shaken for two minutes. The can may be warmed slightly by submerging it in warm (not boiling) water. Build the colour with several coats, allowing them to become touch-dry before respraying. It is also possible to 'flood' the colour over small areas, but this takes practice.

Humbrol enamel paint is available in model shops. It is used for painting metal, plastic and wood and has its own gloss finish (as well as matt) so it does not need lacquering. It is fairly difficult to use for painting fine detail, unless you use a thinning agent. Being oil-based, it takes longer to dry than a water-bound paint. It is cleaned by white spirit or lighter fuel.

Other Finishing Effects

Before a finish is applied, the work should be sanded down lightly when dry.

Wax polish is used on bare wood to enhance its appearance, but it offers little or no protection by itself. It makes an excellent finish, however, when applied to thin protective coats of lacquer, polyurethane or sanding sealer. Liberon offers a good range, as does Briwax.

Bleaching lightens the tone of woods and can be done using a commercial bleach from a hardware store or supermarket.

Note: this product is dangerous and you should wear rubber gloves and an apron, as it will burn skin and ruin clothing on contact. If you put bleach on paintbrushes it will destroy the bristles or sables. Bleaches are sometimes sold in two parts with a neutralizer to stop the action of the bleach. Follow the safety instructions. Never put bleach in a metal container. Keep it in the plastic container in which it is sold.

VARNISHING AND LACQUERING

Varnish and lacquer primarily provide protection for the painted surface, and darken and enhance matt water-based paints such as Plaka. With brush application, especially on bare wood, you should lay the first coat across the grain and finish off by brushing along the grain.

Whether you use a brush or spray it is an advantage to make yourself a varnishing and lacquering board, say 305 × 254mm (12 × 10in), with little 6mm (¼in) thick blocks of irregular lengths, spaced at intervals to support the pieces to be varnished or lacquered, so that they don't stick to the board.

Do not load on too much varnish or lacquer, or it will run on to the underside of the work. Lightly sand between each coat with a fine abrasive, if you want a really smooth finish.

Varnish or lacquer applied to printed ephemera should be lightly sprayed, not brushed, as this would dissolve and disturb oil- or spirit-based printing ink. Carry out a preliminary test to ensure that the medium is compatible. An initial light spray or two will fix the printed surface and render it safe for brush application when it is dry. Never apply a second (or, indeed, any subsequent) coat too soon, otherwise cockling and wrinkling may occur.

Varnish consists of a mixture of copal gums and linseed oil mixed with turpentine. It is slow-drying but can give a very pleasant finish. Ronseal Clear Varnish is a tough polyurethane varnish for interior wood, which is touch-dry in two to four hours between coats. A matt varnish could be considered if the pieces may be photographed.

Quick-drying nitro-cellulose lacquer is available in sprays or tins. Cellulose, made chiefly of cotton fibre, is mixed in a solution with various chemicals such as plastics and resins to give greater flexibility. It is hard and water-resistant (although not waterproof), but it is not as hard-wearing as synthetic lacquer.

Synthetic lacquer comes in polyester, polyurethane, urea formaldehyde and melamine. These chemicals are very tough and durable, being the strongest on the market. As with most lacquers, it comes in gloss, matt, semi-gloss or eggshell finish.

CLEANING

Clean brushes with soap and lukewarm water for water-bound paints and use white spirit or lighter fuel for oil- or spirit-bound mediums. In both cases, brushes should be finally washed with soap and rinsed in tepid water. Ensure that all trace of pigment has gone as otherwise the brushes will harden. Spirits are used to clean some products such as B-I-N Primer Scaler.

BIBLIOGRAPHY

Some of the following titles may be out of print but may be found in libraries and second-hand bookshops.

Bacon, M., *No Strings Attached* (Virgin, 1997; ISBN 1 85227669x)
An account of Jim Henson's Creature Shop and details of the application of Animatronics in films.

Bailly, C. with Bailly, S., *Automata – The Golden Age 1848–1914* (Sotheby's Publications, 1987; Philip Wilson Publishers Ltd; ISBN 0 85667 345 5)

Bartholemew, C., *Mechanical Toys* (Hamlyn, 1979; ISBN 0 600 363 317)

Bishop, R. and Coblenz, P., *A Gallery of American Weathervanes and Whirligigs* (E P Dutton, New York, 1981; ISBN 0 525 93151 1)

Brown, H.T., *507 Mechanical Movements* (first published 1868; US edition published by Lindsay, 1984; ISBN 991791 425 2)

Carrea, R., *Androids – The Jaquet-Droz Automatons* (Scriptar SA, Lausanne, 1979; ISBN 2 88012 0187)

Chapuis, A. and Droz, E., *Automata: A historical and technological study* (originally published by Editions du Griffon, Neuchatel, Switzerland,1958; translated into English by Alec Reid, and published by Central Book Co. Inc., New York; ISBN unknown)

Cielisk, J. and M., *Lehmann Toys: The History of E P Lehmann 1881–1981* (New Cavendish Books, undated; ISBN 0 904568 40 7)

Fowler and Horsley, *Collins CDT (Technology)* (Collins Educational, 1988; ISBN 0 00327 434 9)

Hillier, M., *Automata and Mechanical Toys* (Jupiter Books, 1976; ISBN 904041 328; Bloomsbury Books, 1998; ISBN 1 87063 0270)

Hulten, P. and Tinguely, J., *A Magic Stronger Than Death* (Thames and Hudson, 1987; ISBN 0 50027 489 4)

Levy, A. (ed.), *The Great Toys of Georges Carette* (New Cavendish Books, 1975; ISBN 0 904568 02 4)

Lipman, J., *Calder's Universe* (Viking, New York, in co-operation with the Whitney Museum of American Art, 1976; ISBN 0670 19966 4)
Showing Calder's 'Circus' in detail.

Marchand, F., *The History of Martin Mechanical Toys* (English edition) (Editions L'Automobiliste 1987; ISBN 2 86941 040 9)

Onn, A.L., and Alexander, G., *Cabaret Mechanical Movement* (Cabaret Mechanical Theatre, 1998; ISBN 0 9528729 0 0)
See also Cabaret's website at www.cabaret.co.uk/

Peppé, R., *Rodney Peppé's Moving Toys: With Complete Plans for Every Toy* (Evans Brothers Ltd, 1980; ISBN 0 237 449668)

Spilhaus, A. and K., *Mechanical Toys: How Old Toys Work* (Robert Hale, 1998; ISBN 0 7090 3857 7)

Spooner, P., *Spooner's Moving Animals* (Virgin, 1986; ISBN 0 86369 175 7) (published by Abrams in USA)

Tate Gallery Exhibition Catalogue, *Tinguely* (Tate Gallery Publications Department, 1982; ISBN 0 905005 78 3)

Basic Machines and How They Work (Dover Publications, 1971; ISBN 0 48621 709 4)

INDEX

abrasives 53
additional mechanisms 114–15
adhesives 54
advertising automata 15
Alexander, Gary 37–8
Alexander, Sarah 39
Alexandrian School 10
androids 11
Aquinas, St Thomas 11
Archimedes 10, 106
automaton 7–8, 12, 15

Bacon, Roger 11
bearing 78
bearings box (making) 78–9
bell crank 94–6, 114–15
Benn, Ernest 34
Benn, Timothy 34
Bentine, Michael 8
Bing, Gebrüder 12
Bontems, Blaise 12
box of mechanisms 109–10
    contents 111

Cabaret Mechanical Theatre 7, 9, 37, 40,
    46, 131, 143
Calder, Alexander 7, 9, 29–30, 39, 137
cams 7, 17, 21, 35, 40, 80–3
    eccentric 80–2
    lobed 80–1
    profile 80
    radial surface 80
    snail 80
    templates 80–1
Carette, Georges 15
Casson, Lucy 20–2, 43
Caus, Solomon de 11
circus 13–15, 29–30, 34, 126, 135, 144
clocks, automated 8, 10–11

cathedral 10
water 10
weight driven 10
clockwork tableaux 17
commissions 8–9, 36, 141–3
conversion table 116
coupler bar 92
crank 7, 43, 84–6, 88, 92
    throw of 88
crank pin 78, 84, 98, 114–15
crank slider 84–7, 92
    circular bearing 84–5
    peg board 84–7
    slotted bearing 84–5
crankshaft 78–9, 84–5, 106–7
    double 86, 88–90
Ctesibius 10
cutting mat (calibrated) 88
cycle 8, 83, 96

Decamps, Ernest 12
decline of automata 15
Descartes, René 11
design 128–9, 141–4
drilling 64
drive 98–100
    chain and sprocket 99–100
    friction 99–100
    positive 99–100
Duchamp, Marcel 29
dwell 81, 98

eccentric disc 112–13
Eden Project 8
Emett, Rowland 8, 40
Euclid 10

film projector 98
folk art 16, 22, 32, 34, 59, 144

disc 80, 82, 84
  pin 80, 84
  roller 80, 83–4
four-bar linkage 92–4
  quadratic crank 92
French prisoners of war models 12
friction driven pole 104–5, 78
friction fit 78, 90
  fitting pegs 1, 27, 66
fulcrum 94, 106
Fuller, Ron 7, 22–4, 37, 141, 143–4

gears 7, 100–2
  cogwheels 100
  friction-driven discs 100
  pin wheels 78, 101, 103–4
Geneva wheel, or stop 98–9, 114–15
Golden Age 11–12
Gould, Jack 22
Grayson, John 25–7

Hardy, Neil 40–2
Hazell, Andy 37–8, 43–5
Hero of Alexandria 10–11
Hunkin, Tim 9, 37–8, 46–8
hydraulic automata 10–11

Jackson, Sue 7, 37–9, 143
Jackson, Will 8
Jacquet-Droz, Henri Louis 11
jaquemarts (jacks) 10
jumping jack 16, 30, 32, 119, 129–30

kits 37, 77
Klee, Paul 55, 141
Knipe, Tim 39

Lacey, Bruce 8
Lambert, Leopold 12
Lehmann, Ernest P. 15, 19
Leschot, Jean Frederic 12
levers 7, 17, 40, 70, 88–90, 94, 105–9
  orders of 106
  plain 107–9
  slotted 107–9
linkage mechanisms 7, 90–4
  bar 90–1
  bell crank 94–5

four-bar 92–3
living pictures 17
Lucie-Smith, Edward 32

Magnus, Albertus 11
Maillardet, Jean David 12
Maltby, John 55–7
Mann, Tony 58–60
Markey, Peter 7, 35, 37, 60–2, 77, 141, 143
Marklin, Gebrüder 15
Martin, Fernand 16
McKay, Ian 4, 67–9
mechanical advantage 106
Meggendorfer, Lothar 18
miniature mechanisms 112–13
motion 92, 94, 96
  intermittent, or stepped 96
  oscillating, or reciprocating 86, 91–2, 94, 114–15

Nelson, Frank 7, 9, 29, 35, 70–2
Newstead, Keith 37, 73–5
Nicholson, Ben 55

Parnham House 36, 70
pawl 96, 114–15
Pentagram Partnership 8, 34
Peppé, Rodney 117–19
Phalibois, Jean Marie 12
Philo, the Byzantian 10
Picasso, Pablo 131
pin wheel 78, 101, 103–4
  pitch circles 101, 104
pivot stand 89–90
Plimmer, Martin 39
powered automata 7, 9
printed tin plate 25, 135, 145
prototype 141
puppets 8, 32, 34–5, 151

Race, Robert 120–2
radial surface 80
rainforest materials 9
ratchet 7, 78, 96–8
  intermittent, or stepped, motion 96
  pawl 96, 114–15
Renou, Louis 12

Ride of Life 21, 38–9
Robinson, William Heath 8
robot 12, 29
Rouault, Georges 154
Roullet, Jean 12
Roullet et Decamps 12
Rose, Muriel 32
Rose, Yootha 22

sanding 66
Schoenhut, Albert 17–18
Serpentine Gallery 34, 67, 70
shaft 7, 78–9
    crankshaft 78–9, 84–5, 106–7
    double crankshaft 86, 88–90
Shaw Ashton, Dudley 33
Smith, Martin 123–5
Smith, Matt 37
Smith, Sam 7–9, 22, 30–7, 39, 67, 70, 73,
    117, 143, 154–5
Spooner, Paul 7–8, 29, 37–8, 77, 131–3,
    141–3
spring 80, 96–7, 112–13
Strauss, Fernand 19
string-operated toys 16–19
style 142–3, 154

technique 63
Théroude, Alexander 12

Tinguely, Jean 7, 9, 30
tinplate toys 15–16, 19, 25
Tomlinson, Melanie 134–6

Van Gogh, Vincent 154
varnishing and lacquering 156
Vaucanson, Jacques de 11
Vichy, Gustave 12
Villardebo, Carlos 29

Wain, Louis 17
Wallis, Alfred 55
Westermann, H.C. 67
Whirligig 16, 34, 117
Williams, Kit 8
Williamson, Eric and Alison 61, 77
Wilson, Douglas 29, 137–9
wind-up toys 7, 19
Wood, Vicki 148–50
Wyatt Smith, Kristy 145–7

Zalud, Jan 37, 151–3

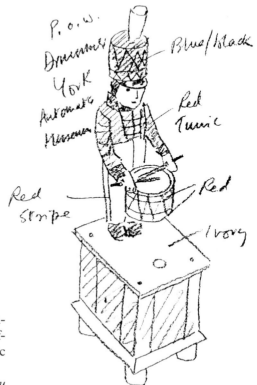

If a man does not keep pace with his com-
panions, perhaps it is because he hears a different drummer. Let him step to the music
he hears, however measured or far away.
Henry David Thoreau